Praise

'When I read this book, I wanted to get started right away. *The Athlete's Ascent* teaches you the fundamentals of creating flow to enhance the quality of your sporting movements. The book is structured in such a way that it provides you with the right keys and choices to perform your best under pressure, and the why and how are clearly explained. I recommend this book for every player who takes their sports performance seriously. This work is special – for most athletes, it will be the key to achieving the best results.'

— **Patsy van Baarle-van Rompaey**, PGA Advanced Professional, Master Performance Coach, elite horse rider (Belgian title, early 1980s), Belgian national elite surfer (1990–2001)

'Jayne's is a voice that is sorely needed in the world of sport performance, and I applaud her for the courage to speak to this need and to do so in such a coherent and effective manner. *The Athlete's Ascent* is required reading for all the athletes I work with, as it provides a touchstone for the core ideas surrounding sport and performance that challenge traditional approaches. Jayne's work speaks to that beautiful and complex space in sport where mind and body unite to create effortless movement – a space that is hard to describe and commodify and, as such, a space that is seemingly counter-current. This is an engaging and practical book, outlining key philosophical arguments for the need for new approaches and perspectives, and offering strategies and systems to cultivate the habits required to adopt this new paradigm and approach to performance. As in her earlier work, Jayne masterfully blends Eastern philosophies with Western ideology to create a unique and novel opportunity for athletes to excel under pressure.'

— **Jon Roy**, Canadian performance coach, recognised for creativity and excellence over twenty-five years, with a passion for mindset architecture across all sport

'To achieve high performance and enter "the zone" or "flow state", the ability to control the biochemistry and inhabit the present moment are the biggest challenges facing athletes, as they require a level of attention that goes beyond the traditional mental game. In *The Athlete's Ascent*, Jayne Storey not only explains for our better understanding how brain–body chemistry affects movement in sport, but offers a solid practice based on her many years of personal experience. Once adhered to, her methods will bring you the Gold. You need to dive in and do the training in order to find out for yourself.'

— **Andy Knibbs**, tennis coach and Inner Game Global Facilitator

'To perform at our highest level, we need to take a holistic approach. *The Athlete's Ascent* is a refreshing journey that will help readers get out of their own way when facing the most intense pressure. Jayne does a wonderful job of exploring concepts that have helped humans perform at their best for thousands of years. If you want to take your game to the next level, this book should be part of your toolkit.'

— **Jon Sherman**, author of *The Four Foundations of Golf*

'What do Tiger Woods, Tom Brady, Novak Djokovic, Michael Jordan, Kobe Bryant, and JJ McCarthy all have in common, other than being the very best at their respective sports? They all have a daily meditation practice. This allows them to be more aware of their mind–body relationship when the pressure's on. As a former PGA Golf Professional, I can say that while most of us are not blessed with the physical tools these elite athletes have, we can all practise the techniques Jayne lays out in *The Athlete's Ascent* to improve our own performance. After reading this book and working with Jayne, I feel strongly that the difference between the above-mentioned sportsmen and the hundreds they have competed against is the ability to quieten the mind in the biggest moments. This helped them to win more consistently against their peers, often by the slimmest of margins. This book gives you the road map to do the same thing. If competing at your maximum level more often is important to you, *The Athlete's Ascent* will be critical for your success.'

— **David Collins**, former PGA Golf Professional, Florida

'If you are an athlete who regularly participates in competitive sport, *The Athlete's Ascent* is a must-read. You will begin to fully understand why many players have become lost in one of two areas: either they are drowning in "technical" thinking, trying to perfect movement through conscious direction, or they have become consumed by attempting to "think correctly" as a result of much of the current psychology literature. Both approaches will leave you short of your true potential – a potential that is released when you understand more about the mind–body connection and the genius of the body when it is allowed to flow naturally. Jayne's work is the embodiment of someone who has applied herself over many years to diligent daily practice. In this book she offers no promise of ridiculous shortcuts but invites you to commit to the path of mastery. If you read this fantastic work and then apply the wisdom contained in these pages, you will make a significant difference not only to the sport you play but, perhaps more importantly, to the life you lead.'

— **Karl Morris**, performance coach and owner, The Mind Factor

'As a novice golfer in my fifties, starting a new sport was daunting. So I was excited and relieved to read in *The Athlete's Ascent* that I would already have learned many of the movements needed for golf, through other sports I have played throughout my life. The years spent turning and breathing around a longitudinal axis in competitive swimming, or gripping for sheer life on edges at 40 miles per hour on a line I'd committed to at the top of the ski hill, or simply running up the spiral stairs with too many bags as a kid, feeling the force throw me up and in, as I went around – my joined-up bodymind can handle all these moves. So I can trust it will be the same with a golf swing. I just have to learn to stay out of the way, and in this book, Jayne expertly provides all the tools and practices needed to do this.'

— **Katie Bayne**, multidisciplinary athlete, Atlanta, Georgia

THE ATHLETE'S ASCENT

DEEP PRACTICE AND HIGH PERFORMANCE

JAYNE STOREY

Author of *Breathe Golf*

R^ethink

First published in Great Britain in 2024
by Rethink Press (www.rethinkpress.com)

Cover image © iStock / M_a_y_a; Shutterstock / Real Sports Photos
Illustrations © Tom Harding Illustration, London

Disclaimer: The publisher and the author recommend that you consult with your physician or trainer before beginning any training program. The publisher and the author are not responsible for any injury you may sustain during the course of performing the exercises presented in this book. They advise you to take full responsibility for your safety and consider your suitability for the training, and not to take risks beyond your level of experience, aptitude and comfort level.

'We are centred,
Stable and still as a mountain.
Our chi sinks to the t'an tien,
We are as if suspended from above.
Our spirit is concentrated within and
Our outwards manner perfectly composed.
Receiving and issuing energy are
Both the work of an instant.'
    — 'Song of Central Equilibrium',
      Jan Diepersloot, *Warriors of Stillness*

In memory of my beloved parents

Contents

Foreword   **1**

Introduction   **5**

Rethinking the traditional approach   6

An experience of flow   8

Healing the mind–body split   10

How this book will help   14

PART ONE

A New Look At Performing Under Pressure   **17**

Shifting The Paradigm   **19**

The mental game   21

A new awareness   24

Overcoming Performance Anxiety   **29**

My experience of being in the moment   32

Controlling your biochemistry   36

Performance Practice   **41**

    What should you include?   43

Stillness   **47**

    Learning to surrender   48

    The importance of stillness in preparation   50

Intention   **57**

    Learning from the experts   59

    Tenpin rehearsal   60

Visualisation   **65**

    Sensing the hara   67

    Visual motor rehearsal   68

Flow   **71**

    The holy grail   73

    A formula for flow   76

Natural Movement Principles   **81**

    Allowing the body freedom   83

    Trusting the body   85

Investing In Loss   **91**

    Trust the process   92

PART TWO

Ten Essential Principles Of High Performance   **95**

The Principles   **97**

　Methods for deep practice   99

Principle One: Controlling Your Biochemistry   **105**

　The six areas of the brain   108

　Seated meditation   113

Principle Two: Quietening Your Mind   **119**

　Why apps aren't enough   120

　Breathing into the moment   122

Principle Three: Holding The Centre   **127**

　Working with the t'an tien   129

Principle Four: Relaxed Readiness   **135**

　Standing meditation (*Yiquan*)   137

　The wisdom of Kung Fu   141

　Slow-walking meditation   144

　Slow-motion practice   146

Principle Five: Listening   **151**

　Avoiding stress   152

Principle Six: Self-observation   **155**

    Exercise One: Walking to the first tee   157

    Exercise Two: Sports practice session   158

    Exercise Three: Enhancing your
    performance   159

Principle Seven: Making Time   **161**

    Intentional effort   162

Principle Eight: Just Enough   **165**

    Economy of movement   166

Principle Nine: Wonder And Awe   **169**

    The role of humility   170

Principle Ten: Downtime And Recuperation   **175**

    Reward yourself with joy   177

PART THREE

Twelve-Week Mind–Body Performance Challenge   **179**

Introduction To The Challenge   **181**

    How the challenge was born   183

    The aim of the challenge   186

    Before you begin   188

Week One   **193**

    Week One action plan   196

Week Two   **201**

    Week Two action plan   204

Week Three   **207**

    Cardio workouts   208

    Strength training   210

    Exercises   214

Week Four   **217**

    Week Four action plan   220

Weeks Five To Eight   **225**

    Weeks Five to Eight action plan   229

Weeks Nine, Ten And Eleven   **233**

    Keep going – you're nearly there!   234

    Weeks Nine, Ten and Eleven action plan   238

Week Twelve   **241**

Conclusion   **243**

    Next steps   245

Bibliography   **247**

Acknowledgements   **251**

The Author   **253**

Foreword

For me, an athlete's ascent starts with noticing the unintended yet negative impact a wandering mind can have on performance, especially under pressure. In working with Jayne and her team, I realised that learning how to witness my thought processes rather than being limited by the confines of my own mind could significantly benefit my life. This realisation became one of those moments in life that you can't 'unsee'. It was evident this was the path that would help me grow both personally and professionally.

This book outlines the work and dedication it takes to cultivate experiential knowledge: the kind of knowledge that is earned through a commitment to getting out of your own way with a daily practice of inner quietude so that a higher intelligence can emerge.

When you reflect on what your inner conditions were like during pressure situations, you discover how it felt when you performed at your best or what got in the way when you didn't. It's that feeling of spontaneously crushing the perfect 3 wood on a par 5 by 'setting up from the inside', or seeing the line on a 4 foot putt to win and committing to it, exhaling through the stroke. It's that feeling of standing on the free throw line at the end of a game and trusting in what Jayne calls 'team mind–body' in the same way you did countless times when you trained in your driveway. It's knowing what it feels like to get that jump when you're fully present before the ball is snapped.

Once you experience this higher level of performance, the daily practice Jayne advocates begins to resonate and the real work begins. You start seeing how a connected mind and body can generate a pure source of energy that you never knew existed. As you continue down the path, you start preparing for performance in a new way. You gain comfort from knowing that through your disciplined training you have a new inner ally, and it's not in the form of the mental toughness that everyone talks about but something intrinsic and more profound. You're now equipped to excel in the face of pressure and will be content with the outcome, as there is no ego attachment or judgement or blame, just a return to that inner stillness. The game becomes a journey of personal growth, letting go of negative self-beliefs and being led by an inner knowing rather than thinking.

There are no fixed formulas for any of this, it's a personal path for everyone. The key is bringing to life your inner intelligence, which is sitting quietly inside you and patiently waiting for you to listen. This book serves as a guide to assist this awakening and overcome your self-imposed limitations.

I can feel the shift in our society towards training the quiet mind for enhanced performance, driven by pioneers like Jayne Storey. There will always be a place for technical knowledge and motivational psychology, but as she explains, when the game starts, it's time to apply your daily practice and fully inhabit the present moment.

Ryan Wirth
Adviser at a leading financial and lifestyle advice firm, serving athletes, entertainers, executives and entrepreneurs

Introduction

This book offers the definitive guide to helping you overcome all the symptoms of anxiety and self-interference so that you can perform at your best in competitive sport, especially during those intense moments of pressure like driving off the first tee, a second serve that simply has to go in, or your final chance to impress the judges in your gymnastics floor routine.

Having been extremely shy and self-conscious as a child and young woman, it became my life's mission to find the secret of how to relax and be myself, rather than suffer the agony of awkwardness in social situations. When I took up Tai Chi in the late 1980s, I started to feel more at home in my body, and with the increased confidence and energy this gave me, I began running, cycling and doing circuits in the gym.

This laid the groundwork for developing my twin passions: the martial arts and fitness training, which in turn sparked a lifelong quest to discover how complex athletic skills can be performed in the fluid, powerful and effortless way we see in the meditative and movement traditions of the East.

These traditions can be summed up simply as the Zen arts, which include everything from meditation to Archery, calligraphy and swordplay, and the martial arts of the *Nei Kung*, or internal schools, of which Tai Chi is the most well known.

The principle of how mind, breathing and spontaneous movement coincide in these arts, whether it's through striking an opponent, drawing a sword or even pouring tea, is exemplified by the *Ensō* circle. This is drawn by hand, often in a single brushstroke that expresses a moment in time when the analytical mind withdraws, allowing the body to move freely.

This, in a nutshell, is the holy grail for those who perform under pressure.

Rethinking the traditional approach

The athlete with the quietest mind is *always* the one to exhibit the most fluid movement and find the extra edge needed on those big points. When the thinking mind quietens down, the body can move in the way it's supposed to, with a connected power and grace that emerges naturally in the moment; yet this connected movement can only emerge in an athlete who has trained, honed, and *embodies* certain principles through which technical and mental prowess are unified. This is the way of deep practice which I firmly believe is the one true path leading to a never-ending ascension consistent with continual high performance.

I am now in my late fifties, and even after a lifetime of meditation and an almost daily martial arts practice, I am still discovering the layers and layers of wonder that a more collected state reveals about how complex movement skills can be expressed naturally and effortlessly through the physical body once the trap of the analytical mind has been bypassed.

This undertaking is a long way from 'thinking about thinking' (mental game) and 'thinking about moving' (technique and mechanics), which form the basis of mainstream sports coaching. It presents an emerging paradigm that requires a particular form of training, or Performance Practice, to help the athlete bridge the gap between mind and body, idea and action, intention and movement.

When the emphasis is placed mainly on the mind, as it is in the conventional approach, there is a great disparity between how an athlete practises and prepares to compete and how this shows up in their sport. In other words, the practice-to-performance ratio, which weighs up the hours spent training against the level of skill executed in competitive situations, clearly shows a problem that hasn't yet been solved.

Athletes failing to live up to expectation are encouraged to toughen up mentally, spend more time in the gym, seek the help of a psychologist and maybe change their technical coach, yet none of this acknowledges or addresses the fundamental split between the mind and body, the default condition of the human being, which can only be reconciled through an intentional redirection of the attention towards the breathing and the physical being.

This deep practice has hitherto been missing from sports, and the current approach exacerbates and widens the mind–body split. Before we go any further, it is helpful to backtrack a little to see how the new paradigm first revealed itself.

An experience of flow

Around the turn of the millennium, due to the feedback I was getting from my Tai Chi students, who commented that the regular classes they were attending were helping them to improve their recreational golf, competitive swimming and holiday skiing, I decided to investigate.

I soon discovered that the meditative state attained when practising Tai Chi and its related arts is a direct parallel to the state of 'flow', an idea first coined by Mihaly Csikszentmihalyi, which athletes experience in those moments of excellence like the pure golf shot, a fearless slalom ski run or the perfect underwater turn in the middle of a freestyle race. It then became my overarching mission to bring this training to athletes who want to practise and apply centuries-old wisdom to high-performance sports.

I felt that people who love sport would inherently understand the necessity of this approach and would benefit from a way to experience flow more often. I had enjoyed these moments myself, not only when practising Tai Chi but also during my regular fitness training.

One morning, I was running through an unfamiliar park and as I came around the bend through the trees, I saw an almighty hill in front of me with two dozen or more steps cut into the terrain. What was so noticeable about this moment of being in flow was that there was no inner dialogue about how hard it was going to be to run up this monstrosity, and nothing in my internal state changed upon seeing it. My mind, body and breathing remained unified, and I continued to run, one stride at a time, up the steps to the top of the hill and down the other side and on through the trees.

It's this relationship between inner quiet and the fluidity or connectedness of movement that we're going to explore. What you're *not* going to find in this book are any psychological or mind-led techniques with their emphasis on positive thinking and reframing negative thoughts. You won't even find anything about the latest trend in mindfulness.

As useful as these interventions are for business and general life, they do little to enhance the performance of complex sporting movement, particularly when the stakes are high and the opponent is an athlete of equal technical ability and fitness.

In these situations, analytical thinking only increases the separation of the mind from the body, and this, above all else, is the reason why so many great athletes fail to perform at their best in pressure situations.

Let me explain.

Healing the mind–body split

The fundamental dichotomy facing all athletes is that the mind loves to think and the body loves to move; yet thinking about how you're thinking or, even worse, thinking about how you're going to move when you swing the club or kick the ball in a few moments widens the fundamental disconnection and results in all the common faults like mistiming, poor contact, lack of tempo, tightness, rushing, loss of balance and so forth.

It's only when mind and body connect – when they are more related or, more specifically, when the mind's awareness can be anchored in a physical sensation like breathing, awareness of the centre of gravity or feeling the feet on the ground – that the movement released will be free, natural, spontaneous and perfectly apt for the situation.

Two questions then arise:

1. How can the mind be helped to quieten down and relinquish the control it wants to have on everything, complex motion included?

2. How can the mind stay with the body rather than being stuck in the trap of its own making, which often sees the same thought patterns repeated over and over, day by day?

This is where the training in this book is going to help you.

For now, it's important to see that the mind and the body have different functions, different jobs or roles; they even operate at different speeds, and yet in conventional coaching the assumption remains that the mind can organise and control movement. It cannot. The mind can no more take over the role of the body and perform the functions of the physical body than the body can take over the functions of the mind, and their increasing separation in the midst of competition will inevitably lead to a collapse of form.

An experienced athlete relying on technical prowess or an equally experienced athlete with a degree of mental toughness can each fare well, until the moment pressure comes into the equation. Then, in both instances, analysis takes over, the breath gets shallower, the stress response kicks in and the mind begins overanalysing, trying to 'get it right'.

As such, it ends up working *against* the body, trying to control and organise movement, which throws up the common mistakes we see in all sports from basketball to surfing. Two of the worst-case scenarios are the 'yips' in golf and 'choking' in other sports, and we've seen plenty of examples of these, even from athletes at the world-class and Olympic levels.

Unlike the mind, the body is designed to process energy through the air you breathe and the food you eat and to move you through your life; it loves free expression and responding to natural laws of motion like gravity and spin, which form the basis of many sporting pursuits, including running, jumping, kicking a ball, hitting a ball with a club or racket, skiing down a mountain and diving into the water.

When the mind and body work together, everything from large expansive movements to the finest, subtlest details come together beautifully. The experience is often effortless, a word I've heard used time and again by athletes of all ages, all disciplines and all levels to describe a particular quality that occasionally just seems to happen.

The problem when performing in high-pressure situations is the tendency to try and force things, to start thinking too much and attempting to use the mind to influence motion with the conventional approach of reframing thoughts and thinking about your technique.

As you're no doubt aware, the harder you try and the more active your mind, the more disjointed or disconnected your movement becomes. Conversely, athletes who have begun the daily work of deep practice and have started to embody certain principles, which we'll look at in depth together in Part Two of the book, have enjoyed greater freedom of movement and the ability to calmly execute their movement skills while under tremendous pressure.

The alternative paradigm posited here is to develop a Performance Practice, the aim of which is three-fold. First, you have to *see* the fundamental disconnection and the fact that, for the most part, sport is dominated by your thoughts; second, you must train to establish and strengthen the mind–body connection and, by making a particular and consistent effort, not let the mind hijack your attempts. Third, you begin to embody certain inner conditions in preparation and performance that allow you to enter the realm of flow more often in the midst of competition.

From the feedback I've received from hundreds of clients who've been training to do just this, it is clear to me that the quality of the athlete's inner state, whether anxiously disjointed or calmly collected, ranges on an imaginary performance scale from control-freak mind (CFM) at one end to team mind–body (TMB) at the other.

This shows up not only when the athlete is in motion, but also in the moments *before* movement begins, and, as we'll discover, it is what renders ball striking, backflips and bowling either clumsy and inept or powerful and precise.

How this book will help

This book was written as a way of reaching out beyond golf to athletes involved in many other sports to help spread this new paradigm to all those who want to achieve their physical, mental and sporting potential, especially in competition. It is also a response to seeing so many people who love sport failing to make the most of their skills and their dedication to training while competing, simply by misunderstanding what's necessary to deliver fluid movement when they are under pressure.

The Athlete's Ascent presents a brief but essential guide to how you can benefit from the turning tide in sports performance, which is seeing more and more athletes, from elite level to grassroots enthusiasts, turn to meditation and other Eastern practices like Tai Chi and Yoga as part of their training, believing these disciplines can help them stay calm under pressure and triumph over their opponents.

As one of the early pioneers of this new genre which seeks to apply Eastern philosophy and practice to high-performance sports, I have been encouraging athletes to develop a deep practice to help unify mind, body and movement since the turn of the millennium.

In this book you will benefit from many long years of work and research and learn how to apply your practice in real-time pressure situations. I will give you Ten Essential Principles of High Performance to hone this new paradigm into a daily Performance Practice as well as a unique Twelve-week Mind–Body Performance Challenge to help you make it part of your sports training routine, and I will intersperse the text with drills and 'try this' activities to embed your learning.

This approach will help you to overcome nerves, anxiety and mental interference – the three main stumbling blocks to performing under pressure that no amount of technical know-how or mental game interventions have been able to fully resolve.

The book offers a solution that will quieten the mind and bring it into closer unity with your breathing and your physical body, taking into account a vast and ancient backdrop that includes much of the philosophy, principles and practices of traditional Eastern disciplines from Archery to Tai Chi and Zen meditation.

It will help you understand and develop a Performance Practice so that you know exactly what to include in your day-to-day routine, skill development and preparation for performance, and learn to apply it in the heat of the moment to express your love of sport in the most natural and spontaneous way possible.

PART ONE

A NEW LOOK AT PERFORMING UNDER PRESSURE

'People who know the state of emptiness will always be able to dissolve their problems by constancy.'
— **Shunryu Suzuki**, *Zen Mind, Beginner's Mind*

Shifting The Paradigm

Let's take a closer look at why sports performance so desperately needs a new paradigm. Herein lies the rub: many athletes have a cursory interest in meditation and, intellectually at least, they can understand the benefits. Some, of course, especially those at the top of their game, commit to some form of regular practice; however, for the vast majority this remains little more than listening to guided imagery on mindfulness using a smartphone app. If this sounds like you, read on to find out why this approach might not be helping as much as you would like and why it's necessary to take the next step.

In golf, it's well known that Tiger Woods, winner of fifteen majors, has been a lifetime practitioner of meditation and learned Tai Chi as a youngster. In tennis, Novak Djokovic, winner of twenty-four Grand Slam titles, is also dedicated to his meditation practice and spends time at a Buddhist temple in London when competing at Wimbledon. In the women's game, Bianca Andreescu stunned spectators when she defeated all-time great Serena Williams to win her first Grand Slam title in 2019. The nineteen-year-old credited much of her success to her practices of Yoga and meditation. There are many more examples like this at the elite level, from the late, great Kobe Bryant in basketball to Olympic, world and European champion of the women's long jump, Malaika Mihambo, who has spoken about her use of meditation as a key part of her pre-competition preparation.

The vast majority of sportspeople seeking to embrace these traditions, however, remain stuck with a foot in each of two worlds, both of which, on the surface, might seem related to formal practice but are, subtly, miles away: first, the world of modern mindfulness, and second, the world of psychology and the so-called mental game. Rarely do they embark on a deeper exploration of what it means to quieten the mind and experience how this enhances the release of complex movement skills.

As such, in a pressure situation, the overriding tendency is to abandon any tentative attempts made towards inner quietude, such as awareness of breathing, in favour of positive thinking or reviewing one's technique ahead of the next strike or ball toss, believing that it will be more conducive to producing a winning shot. In crunch moments, without the support of a consistent and disciplined approach – a deep practice – most athletes will revert to the thinking mind, lacking confidence in the internal stillness that spells the difference between being the champion or the runner-up.

The mental game

The mental game and technical thinking are endorsed by some of the world's top coaches and reiterated by television commentators the world over, despite the fact that these approaches can so easily overspill into the analysis paralysis characteristic of the CFM. Indeed, mental interference is one of the main stumbling blocks athletes face when trying to execute their craft, especially in the heat of competition, and yet the onus in mainstream sports is invariably on having the mind think about thinking or think about movement.

This default tendency in all sport and at all levels (despite growing evidence to the contrary) dismisses the inner world of quiet connectedness in favour of mental toughness and technical know-how. The reason for this is because hitherto there has been little understanding of, or a way of expressing in language, how and why the true meditative state, which is so akin to the zone, or flow, serves the athlete's ability to release their fundamental movement skills when it matters.

This is the crux of the matter and the issue that's been my raison d'être for almost three decades. Many coaches have written and spoken about how to help athletes perform under pressure and have offered umpteen suggestions based on a cursory understanding of breathing 'techniques' and ideas about the mind–body connection. These approaches aren't necessarily helping, because they remain based within psychological parameters rather than a deeper understanding emerging from a dedicated practice.

It seems that this trend seeks to encompass many other fields in its approach, purporting to help not only those who love sport but also businesspeople, college students and public speakers. It seems clear, therefore, that by neglecting to home in on specifically *what* athletes are required to perform under pressure, ie complex movement, these one-size-fits-all approaches do a great disservice to those who want to reach their potential on the tennis court, golf course, halfpipe, balance beam and so on.

What I've learned is that when complex sporting movement is the issue, the mind is almost invariably the enemy. In fact, the only way the mind can have any positive influence on the natural expression of movement is when it is subdued.

When paradigms shift there is always a crossover period when the new ideas are first ridiculed, then opposed and undermined by the mainstream before finally being taken as self-evident. I see this time as a definite crossover from the old-world paradigm which has been about thinking (mental and technical) to this new world which is about *connecting* (mind, breathing and movement).

As we're discovering, the fading authority of the conventional approach coaches the mind and body, or the mental game and technical game, separately, and it views mindfulness as an adjunct to psychology. It therefore fails to acknowledge the importance of inner quietude, even though athletes who have experienced flow have described this level as being clearly beyond the thinking mind.

The emerging ethos outlined in this book sees the mind–body connection as the all-important, overarching condition necessary for enabling complex movements like the golf swing, the jump shot or the triple Salchow in figure skating to be delivered with fluidity and precision. It seeks to help athletes train this state of inner connectedness with disciplines and practices that transcend the psychological boundaries which can trap them in a limited expression of their full capabilities.

A new awareness

To begin your ascent towards consistently higher performance, you need to look closely to see if you can appreciate the inherent disconnection you face from moment to moment. You will then set about training to narrow this gap so that TMB can come to the fore in those moments that matter.

TRY THIS: Grounding awareness

Bring your awareness into your feet, specifically trying to feel the sensation of your soles on the ground or your feet enclosed within your shoes. Aim to keep a relaxed but steady attention on either foot or both your feet as you read the rest of this chapter. This sounds easy but may be more difficult than you imagine.

Most likely after only a few moments you will no longer be attentive to the sensation of your feet within your shoes and the ground beneath them, and your mind will have resumed its habitual thinking, such that you lose the fragile connection to the awareness you began the exercise with.

You can try this again several times throughout the day – as often as you remember.

If you tried the above exercise, you'll have noticed how quickly and easily the mind gets distracted and shifts away from even the remotest connection to the body, reverting to its customary patterns of thinking – curiously, without you even noticing.

We could talk for hours about why this is so, using examples from science and philosophy to religion and esoterica, but the point we're concerned with is this: in mainstream sports the inherent mind–body disconnection is actively trained and encouraged as part of an athlete's preparation for and execution of their skills, as it's mistakenly assumed that the mind can control movement.

A golfer, tennis player or gymnast will enter the game or competition believing their positive thoughts and knowledge of technique can help them deliver the perfect drive, sublime forehand pass or backflip, only to find when pressure enters the equation that the analytical mind dominates and the mind–body split becomes a widening chasm.

Under pressure, the breathing changes, anxiety is induced, the nervous system switches into stress mode, the worry mind gets overactive, and this self-interference renders movement clumsy and inept so that even the greatest players in the world will slam a return shot into the net despite an open court or start searching for a swing on the final tee in a golf tournament.

I've worked with athletes from many different sports, the vast majority of whom have benefitted from a daily Performance Practice which trains the mind–body connection, and they have recognised a similar state in meditation to when they've been in flow.

They describe a heightened clarity, relaxed attention, a sense of knowing rather than thinking, feeling calm but strong, and a keen awareness that the intention for movement will be perfectly executed with precision, power and grace by the physical body.

Most of my clients are golfers who suffer with an inordinate amount of technical overload, which exacerbates the Worry Brain, especially when under pressure. I have also worked with tennis players and swimmers as well as those who love cycling, gymnastics, figure skating, motor racing, equestrianism, snowboarding and skiing, endurance and extreme sports, middle-distance running and more.

Having researched their histories, coached them and listened to the feedback from my clients from junior to club level and elite to world-class for over thirty years, it's my firm conviction that the fundamental issues affecting performance in high-pressure moments are the same for *every* athlete.

It's not the particular sport that's in question, it's the fact that anyone involved in sport has to perform a series of complex movements which are either connected, seamless and effortless when the mind and body come together, or disconnected, inelegant and off-target when the mind and body are divided.

As such, the unique approach of having a Performance Practice – which, as we'll see, can help you to emulate the conditions that exist when flow appears – is of paramount importance no matter what your sport or level of achievement thus far. If you are looking to reach your potential and win against other athletes of equal physical and mental ability, this will become the missing link in your arsenal.

TMB needs training and it cannot be the same training as that which encourages CFM, by which I mean it's not about more thinking, positive self-affirmations or the million and one things you know about the mechanics of your sport. It's about bringing a state of quiet equanimity to the inner world which allows movement to emerge naturally, spontaneously and freely in the moment.

One of the main factors affecting the quality of this inner connectedness is the athlete's biochemical response to perceived pressure; in other words, what happens to the brain, breathing and nervous system under duress and how this triggers mental interference even though it's assumed that negative thoughts arise first. They don't.

Inside every athlete, regardless of their sport, the nervous system is triggered into a particular state according to a hardwired range of responses which either restrict movement (when the stress response is activated) or enable the release of natural, instinctive movement (when the relaxation response is triggered).

As the problem is the same for each individual athlete, so the solution is the same across all sports. Competitive athletes must learn to quieten the mind by controlling the biochemistry – which can only be done by working with the breath – and, moreover, develop the rare and coveted quality of relaxed readiness found in the martial arts to further assist them in responding freely and naturally in the moment.

Overcoming Performance Anxiety

I n a recent survey of my newsletter readers, I asked for feedback on the question 'What does pressure feel like?' Here are some of the (anonymised) responses:

> 'Knowing how good a player I am, and then not performing at that level in a tournament, sparks off memories of hurt and letting myself down, which makes me upset and can turn into anger, anxiety and then a collapse.'

> 'I have yet to succeed when performing short shots around the green in competitive golf as well as I can when playing on my own. The presence of other players seems to affect my ability and my confidence.'

'I often get a nervous tingling in my gut in competitive situations and, tending to err towards the negative, it honestly feels more like anxiety than excitement.'

'When I'm under pressure my preparation gets too quick.'

'I can't help visualising a negative outcome, which leads me to become very self-conscious.'

'I notice my body tightens, my swing feels weird, and I no longer trust myself.'

'My pressure begins in my stomach. It is in knots, feeling uneasy. My breathing starts to shallow, the tension in my upper body starts to increase and I become very inward-looking to the point that I am completely unaware of my surroundings and the people I am playing with.'

'I become very focused on trying not to do something wrong. There is a loss of freedom in my movements, and I can freeze over the ball with way too many thoughts in my head.'

'Generally, I just overthink and lose my commitment to making the shot.'

'For me, pressure stems from a fear of failure, and I believe that fear sends a message to my mind and body that I'm under attack. My heart rate goes up, my breathing is housed in the upper chest, and I can feel some numbing in my hands.'

'In practice, I can hit some great shots but when I'm in the game I find myself thinking, trying, worrying, remembering and generally feeling uptight, and I can't produce anywhere near the quality of shot-making that I know I'm capable of.'

'When the pressure's on, my mind tends to race ahead, and I can overlook simple tasks and end up making poor decisions.'

Interesting, isn't it, that this feedback is all strikingly similar even though we've heard from golfers, tennis, billiard, hockey and badminton players at both the club and elite level?

The experience or feeling of pressure falls into three main categories:

1. Nerves, stress and anxiety

2. Mental interference

3. An inability to move the body freely

At first glance these issues all seem to stem from negative thoughts, images and mental projections about what's going to happen, or rather what *could* happen, in the future, whether that's your opening tee shot in a competition two weeks hence or the penalty shoot-out about to take place with you as one of the team members chosen to score.

As we'll soon see, this is simply the mind's reaction to a change in its biochemistry, which in turn is affected by a change in the breathing and a subsequent widening of the mind–body disconnection.

My experience of being in the moment

How are you getting on feeling your feet on the ground? Thought so!

With a myriad of mindfulness apps and YouTube videos telling us all about presence and being in the moment, we are mistakenly led to believe that awakening to this state is as easy as ordering a pizza delivery on our phone.

Once you unplug, however, from the mainstream drivel and get serious about this work, you'll see that it requires a consistent effort and a genuine struggle with yourself to strengthen the attention which is usually squandered on external, and often meaningless, distractions. It is only by repetitive daily training (known in the Eastern world as *Abhyasa*) that we can come anywhere close to what's required.

As you know, I've been practising Tai Chi for over three decades and alongside this I've been doing regular daily Zen meditation and am considered by many to be the creator of one of the world's leading methodologies for helping athletes perform under pressure.

Many times, and over many years, I have trained on my own, but I've also had the guidance of some highly experienced teachers who have enabled me on more than one occasion to notice the stark difference between thinking and being.

Many of my clients have also had to learn this subtle but crucial lesson. *Thinking* about your breathing in a pressure situation is of no help at all and only adds to the clutter in the mind. If you meditate regularly, for instance by sitting quietly and following the breath each day for 20 minutes, when you're in a tournament and feeling anxious, you're more able to slow down and deepen the breathing such that it calms the bio-chemistry, quietens the Worry Brain and allows your movement to flow.

Some time ago I had an interesting experience which reaffirmed to me, even after decades of training, that the only way to prepare for a moment of pressure is to be in the moment you're in now.

One evening I received a phone call asking if I would present a short Tai Chi demonstration and lesson to a group in London the next day, as part of a formal day of meditation practice. I knew this wasn't a request I could politely refuse. I also knew that, at such events, plans can change on the day according to the engagement of the participants and that I could be called upon to start the session when I was least prepared.

When I hung up the phone, I spent quite some time fretting about not being late, as it was going to be an early start, and thinking about how I was going to introduce the session, which moves from the Tai Chi form I was going to show the group, how long I was going to spend on each move, what I was going to say about the benefits and the martial applications, how I was going to wrap up the session and so on.

The trouble with being considered an expert – as many of my Professional Golfers' Association (PGA) teaching pro clients will attest to – is that it piles pressure on top of pressure. In the situation I was going to face the next day, I knew that even my decades of experience were nothing in comparison to the formidable presence of older, wiser teachers.

It seemed there was no way I could adequately prepare to demonstrate and share my understanding of Tai Chi in such circumstances, although in all other situations I'm more than confident about my knowledge and abilities.

What came to me that evening was that the only way I could ready myself for what had been asked of me was to remember my practice; instead of thinking about it as a future event, taking place sometime the following day, to try and be right there where I was *at that moment*, sitting on the sofa, in my body and in my breathing, rather than letting my mind take over and imagining all sorts of possible scenarios and outcomes the following day.

The next morning, while getting showered and ready, driving to the venue, having breakfast with the group, even during the actual presentation itself, my attention kept coming and going from the present to the imagined and the fear of what might happen. As such, I had to continually remember to anchor myself in the moment and not let my thoughts get the better of me.

You'll realise as we go through this book together that you must continually strive to follow your breath, feel your feet on the ground and let your mind rest in the centre of gravity. Don't make the mistake of thinking this will come automatically or that trying once or twice will suffice.

Controlling your biochemistry

Let's examine what performance anxiety (often called stage fright) actually is. When you worry about something, your mind becomes even more dominant than it usually is, but that's only part of the picture, as we'll soon see. Simply put, it's the biochemistry which triggers feelings of anxiety, and the ensuing negative thought patterns only serve to reinforce this as the mind seeks consistency with the state of nervousness.

Sitting at home worrying about the upcoming Tai Chi demonstration, I started to experience CFM and had less and less connection to my physical self and my breathing. This caused a change in my biochemistry such that I began to feel anxious and soon started imagining the worst; however, my inner equilibrium was restored when I remembered my training, started to breathe more slowly and felt my feet on the ground.

Although it's difficult to catch oneself and even more difficult to practice, controlling the biochemistry changes how you feel, how you think, and most importantly for athletes, how your body moves.

Here's why.

Think of your nervous system as having three different settings: the stress response (aka fight-flight-freeze), neutral, and the relaxation response.

As a human being, you are a self-regulating organism; therefore, you unconsciously seek coherence such that if you start to feel anxious, the mind will get involved and produce one image or scenario after another as to why you should feel nervous.

These thoughts and mental pictures can be anything from 'Remember when you shanked the ball on this hole', 'Remember how you always mess up your dismount from the high bar' or 'This opponent always beats me'.

The pictures in your mind correspond to the sensations of anxiety and can include fear of what others might think, the negative consequences of messing up your routine, and playing safe instead of going for the shot you want. They can also lead to poor decision-making, lack of clarity around your intention, hesitation and lack of commitment or rushing your preparation.

It becomes impossible to move naturally in this state, as the shots or routines you've perfected and performed so well in practice and rehearsal are nowhere to be found. There is no touch, feel or finesse; your smaller muscles and fast twitch muscles stop firing in perfect sequence; there is a distinct lack of co-ordination and all this gets compounded the harder you try and the more you think about how to perform your technique well.

Where does all this self-interference begin?

As documented in my book *Breathe Golf: The missing link to a winning performance*, performance anxiety, stage fright, the yips, choking and otherwise failing to perform under pressure what you can do easily when nothing's at stake or nobody's watching all begin with a change in the breathing. Working with your breathing will be the cornerstone of your Performance Practice, as it's the linchpin of the whole thing.

For most people, unless they are practising meditation, Chi Kung (Qi Gong) or Yoga, the breathing pattern tends to be quick and short, using only the top part of the lungs. For those with some experience of these arts, or who sing or perform on stage, it can involve the diaphragm, and after more intensive practice the breathing begins to take place in the lower abdomen.

TRY THIS: Focusing on the breathing

Sit quietly for a few moments and notice where you are breathing from right now. Without forcing or changing anything, just follow your breathing with a relaxed attention and notice where it's initiated; it will most likely be the upper part of your chest or the solar plexus.

Now place your hands just below your navel on the t'an tien, or centre of gravity. As you do so, try to settle some of your awareness on this area too. Keeping your back straight and your shoulders and chest as relaxed as possible, breathe in and out smoothly and quietly and see if you can sense a slight expansion and contraction of the lower abdomen as you begin to breathe more deeply.

If you can keep this up for a few moments, you will start to feel calm and mellow, and your mind will become quieter than normal.

Throughout the course of your training, you'll develop an awareness of the symbiotic relationship between your breathing and your mind, noticing that when your breathing is soft, smooth and regular and coming from lower down in your body, your mind will tend to be quiet.

You'll begin to notice the connection between your breathing and your biochemistry and how conscious breathing into your centre reduces the sensations of stress, including nervousness, adrenaline, an increased heart rate, a nervous tummy, shaking legs and all the common signs and symptoms of anxiety which can lead to what one of my readers called the 'collapse'.

Performance Practice

Let's look at what else it means to develop a Performance Practice and why this approach is so different from conventional coaching. Traditionally, techniques used to overcome anxiety are classified into two categories. The first is around problem-solving and overcoming adversity and uses interventions like goal setting and strategic planning of everything from training regimes to game tactics. The second is geared towards helping the athlete's emotional state using relaxation techniques, positive mental images, motivational self-talk and restructuring cognitive behaviour.

In my experience, and according to the feedback from athletes I've worked with, these interventions are all well and good until the game or competition, when they do little to de-stress the nervous system and allow complex movement to flow. Even long-term use of the best conventional techniques isn't enough to stop the athlete's fight-flight-freeze response or help them refrain from making inexplicable mistakes and errors or rushing decisions and preparation.

As one PGA teaching pro explained to me before we started working together, his golf had previously been 'determined entirely by my upper body and brain'. When he started witnessing his breathing in meditation and learned to hold his attention at the centre of gravity, his experience of movement changed. It began to be initiated from much lower down in his body, without any self-interfering thoughts, enabling his swing to flow better, so much so that he's excited about the prospect of returning to competitive play.

As it's a complete change or shift in the paradigm around coaching, one that empowers the athlete to the level of self-reliance in those big pressure points, it would be useful for you to ponder on what having a Performance Practice might mean to you. It might be:

- A daily practice that helps to unite your mind and body

- A practice that develops deep abdominal breathing

- A practice that prepares the inner conditions necessary to enter flow

- A practice that helps to harmonise intention and action

- A practice that dispels nerves, anxiety and self-interference

- A practice that helps quieten your mind and free your body

- A set of exercises and drills that have their origin in the martial and Zen arts

A Performance Practice is *not* a psychological intervention and has nothing to do with either positive thinking or knowledge of technique; it is the regular practice of traditional exercises that strengthen the mind–body connection.

What should you include?

Having a daily Performance Practice is the missing link in an athlete's arsenal and must become part of a holistic regime which includes conditioning, endurance, explosive training, nutrition and supplementation, flexibility, technical prowess and positive self-affirmation. In this way it provides the glue which binds everything else together – mind and body, idea and action, intention and technique, self-belief and self-actualisation – so that sporting movement can be expressed spontaneously and with ease.

The exercises and drills include:

- Formal Eastern practices such as following the breath and staying close to the body
- Traditional stance-keeping practices from the martial arts that develop a keen awareness of the body's alignment, posture and balance
- Centuries-old movement drills that activate the t'an tien for increased centrifugal force and more efficient use of the kinetic chain
- Slow-motion exercises from Tai Chi and Taoist circle walking applied to sport-specific drills such as the open-stance forehand in tennis and the golf swing
- Integrating the Performance Practice with sport-specific technical practice
- Applying the practices as part of a real-time performance process in competitive situations

The purpose of these exercises is to develop a practice which first emulates and encourages access to the flow state, and second strengthens your fundamental movement skills, which, as we'll discover, are the same across all sports.

Developing a Performance Practice is your essential preparation and in-game process for performing at the highest level, whether that's for your local team or on the world stage. Without it, the only recourse available, especially when things aren't going your way and you start rushing and trying too hard to get it right, is to think about how you're thinking and about your technique as you prepare to tee off, receive your opponent's serve or exit the gates at the top of the ski run.

TRY THIS: Journaling

Start a training journal with your goals and aspirations for your sport. You can also record your daily Performance Practice and log your progress.

Your first exercise will be to brainstorm your answers to two questions: 'How will my sport develop without a Performance Practice?' and 'How will my sport develop alongside a daily Performance Practice as I learn to master any and all forms of self-interference currently preventing me from being my best?'

Make sure you dream big, because with the right effort consistently applied, it's going to happen. After working together for a couple of seasons, one of my Ladies Professional Golf Association (LPGA) clients told a BBC reporter that she had already ticked off three of her lifetime ambitions, including playing in the Solheim Cup.

As you're learning, when the thinking mind dominates or you have too strong an intention, the mind–body split widens until the signal intended for the motor system is interrupted by CFM, rendering your movement clumsy and inept. The only way the mind can have a positive influence on the delivery of movement is when it is subdued and brought into relation with the physical breath and being, which then encourages the emergence of TMB.

Stillness

We'll look now at some key performance areas which are often misunderstood in the mainstream, mind-centred approach to coaching. By putting them in the proper context, not only against the backdrop of sport but also with the support of time-honoured principles and disciplines, you can strengthen your belief in this new (although ancient) paradigm of the mind–body connection and understand why the daily effort is so necessary.

Individual personal endeavour is always about going against the default world, which applies an outside-in approach to becoming better at your sport; instead, it advocates taking control of your attention, developing self-awareness and using these qualities to grow from the inside.

Effortless movement often emerges seemingly by chance during those moments when you accidentally enter the zone, or flow state, so you should concentrate your efforts on restoring certain long-forgotten conditions within you that are conducive to this experience and support the outward expression of perfect movement.

Simply put, these conditions are an inner quietude and a relaxed readiness, which you must strengthen in your daily practice and come back to, day by day, hour by hour and moment by moment.

First, let's review how, from this new vantage point, the psychological aspects fall away, leaving you with a simpler and more direct route to releasing complex movement skills in a way that's free, natural and sublime.

Learning to surrender

Inner stillness, or the summoning of a more collected state, is all about connection: in the first instance, connecting the attention to the breath and the physical body, which are prerequisites for quietening the mind. In the Eastern world these approaches are known by various names, including *Ch'an*, Vipassana and Zazen.

Many of the Chi Performance methods are based on the training of the internal martial arts schools of Tai Chi, *Hsing Yi* and Bagua, which teach that stillness and movement should become integrated, forming two sides of the same coin. Movement emerges from stillness and stillness is contained within movement. Indeed, as appears in the book *Warriors of Stillness* by Jan Diepersloot, the master Wang Xiangzhai, has said that 'stillness is the master of motion'.

You need to understand, however, that these states cannot be summoned through willpower or by merely changing the way you think. The overarching paradigm shift is something that takes time to appreciate; it's a journey of transformation that requires a certain amount of personal struggle and an eventual surrender to something higher.

It is not the athlete's role to try and hit the pure golf shot or perform the perfect 360-degree backflip or underwater turn; it's the athlete's job to train a state of quiet equanimity, presence and repose through daily practice. This encourages unity of mind and body, idea and action, enabling access to flow and allowing movement to emerge in the moment.

This daily practice is the *Abhyasa*, or Sadhana, of consistent effort spoken of since Patanjali's Sutras on Yoga 3,000 years ago. It persists today in ashrams, monasteries, temples and the local Karate club, but for the most part is missing from sport.

Inner quietude is the goal, the work to be done, and pure spontaneous expression of the body is the outcome to be enjoyed. Learning to put the mind and the ego to one side and trusting a higher intelligence to work it out for you results in an ascent to ever-higher levels of performance and wonder.

I remember one of my teachers explaining that the experience of being more awake or present in the moment, in a state of flow, is 'on the other side of trying'. As such, it's not something we can make happen using the same approach as when we train in the gym, set goals or increase our bank balance. It is almost *received* from a higher level than the human mind, maybe as a reward or gift for honing the attention and working to keep it steady within oneself. To reiterate, we're not speaking about mental toughness or single-mindedly focusing on something external, but of a relaxed self-awareness that includes the body and breathing.

The importance of stillness in preparation

Nowhere is this more important or useful than in the moments *before* you start moving, and your daily practice will help you to draw your awareness towards your posture, balance, physical centre and breathing, bringing you into a more collected state in your set-up or preparation.

Every fault that shows up in complex sporting movement is already there before the athlete starts moving, and yet in the mainstream approach coaches generally deconstruct technical faults *after* the ball strike, back-flip, goal kick etc. The quality of movement is entirely dependent on the quality of stillness and its allied intention during the preparation for movement, and not on how much an athlete knows or thinks about the technique they are going to perform.

Both stillness and intention (which we'll look at more closely in the next chapter) are component parts of the experience of flow, and one of the main reasons for developing your Performance Practice is because it emulates the conditions that give rise or access to this state in the first place.

Of the hundreds of people I have personally worked with, whether they're junior players competing at their local club or the elite, every single athlete in every different sport uses similar words to describe the experience of flow, such as 'an ease of movement', 'a sense of freedom' and 'a feeling of effortlessness'. It makes sense, therefore, to focus your energy and training time on replicating these internal conditions which can only exist when the mind is quiet.

If stillness is replaced by overthinking and the purity of intention is blocked by running through a checklist or menu of movement positions, allied with thoughts of 'trying to get it right' and the inevitable feelings of tightness and anxiety, movement will always be out of sync.

Unfortunately, even elite athletes, coaches and sports commentators are so caught up in the current paradigm that they constantly refer to athletes in terms of not being mentally tough, of their technique letting them down, of golfers needing to change their swing coach, without any acknowledgement of the relationship between stillness and fluidity of motion.

For the mainstream it's all about the mind; but when you begin your Performance Practice it becomes about switching off the inner dialogue or at least turning down the volume. What's interesting about meditation is that with regular practice the prefrontal cortex, which is the realm of analytical thinking that so easily overspills into CFM, goes offline, helping you to enjoy inner quiet and equanimity.

In the mind-led approach, intention is considered to be a mental construction, but as we're discovering from athletes who've spoken about flow, and as we'll examine more closely in the following chapter, intention is more dependent on the quieter Zen-like inner stillness than it is on the analytical mind.

Imagine for a moment the way a Samurai master prepares to spar with an opponent or the way martial arts film stars like Bruce Lee, Jackie Chan or Jet Li prepare for a fight – you will never see them running over technique in their mind or going through a checklist of things to get right. Instead, they will be forming a strong inner connection and a quiet but steady intention that has nothing to do with thinking, either about technique or 'geeing themselves up' with motivational psychology.

It's the same when athletes perform well and yet, as the following anecdote demonstrates, there are still relatively few sportspeople and even fewer sports fans who understand this concept, let alone show a willingness to commit to a daily practice.

As the late Kobe Bryant said of basketball legend Steph Curry, who is known for having an intense pre-game meditation practice:

> *'He's extremely deadly because he's not up and*
> *not down, not contemplating what's gone before*
> *or thinking about what's coming next, he's just*
> *there. When a player has trained himself to have the*
> *skills and you mix it with this calmness you have a*
> *serious problem.'*

When I discovered that the flow state experienced in sport is on a parallel with the Zen-like mind of the East, I did a lot of research. I found out that the neuroscientists Dr Fred Travis and Dr Harald Harung have led research to study the brainwaves of athletes at the Olympic and world-class levels, and they have proven that the player with the quietest mind will always be the one who outclasses their opponents. Unfortunately, most people would rather quote the science than do the training, and that includes a lot of coaches. Even worse, others will try and kid you

that you can attain this state simply by listening to a mindfulness app.

The success of the Eastern approach exemplified in the phrase 'Stillness is the master of motion' has been proven through sophisticated brain imaging that shows how those who are mentally quiet before taking their shot produce a better quality of ball striking. By extension, the golf swing, penalty kick or edge jump are all dependent on where the athlete is on our imaginary performance scale from CFM to TMB.

The secret to performing under pressure is all about the level of stillness you can attain in your set-up or preparation, because when the mind is quiet and mental interference is put to one side, not only can the body move more freely but it will also respond to the intention you have for the shot you want to make or the move you need to perform.

This holds true not just for individual athletes but also for teams. The latest research shows that when teams practise meditation together, their brainwave patterns fall into the same rhythm and they can read each other's cues more intuitively. This phenomenon is known as 'entrainment', defined in the working paper 'Entrainment: Cycles and synergy in organizational behavior', by Deborah Ancona and Chee Leong Chong, as 'the adjustment or moderation of one behavior either to synchronize or to be in rhythm with another behavior'.

Intention

With such emphasis placed on technical thoughts and the so-called mental game in competitive sport, the control-freak nature of the mind has seeped even into important components of preparation, like intention and visualisation, which have little to do with thinking.

Intention is not a construction of the mind, at least not the analytical part of the mind, and as such it cannot be summoned by going through a checklist of points about body positions or the component, segmented parts of a movement you need to perform in front of the judges or your home crowd.

If we look eastwards again, to the world of Zen and the martial arts, we'll see that intention (known as *Yi* or wisdom mind) is a highly focused form of attention directed towards the required outcome *minus* any internal dialogue about how it will be achieved and void of any emotional investment in the results. *Yi* describes a steady, yet cool, flame born in part from a mind empty of all extraneous thoughts, including of personal ambition and attachment.

You may recall Mr Miyagi's training in the Karate Kid movies, which didn't make much sense to the young boy or girl being bullied until they had honed, practised and quietened their mind under his tutelage to the point where their body simply responded in the moment when facing their opponent in the final battle.

Yi is the state which allows the dueller to draw their sword, cut down their opponent and return the blade to its sheath in a single heartbeat. It is the state which allows an archer to synchronise balance, breathing and centring with the release of the arrow to the target, and the calligrapher to paint the *Ensō* circle in a single, continuous move without self-interfering thoughts.

Athletes are still taught to mentally review the technical aspects of their sport before swinging a golf club or hitting a backhand passing shot, with no learning on how to assume a relaxed but ready posture as per the warrior or artist of the Eastern world. It has been taken for granted that thinking about moving will help the release of complex movement skills, although it's becoming increasingly clear, particularly in sports like golf where the average handicap has not changed in almost forty years despite all the technological advances in ball and club manufacturing, that nothing could be further from the truth.

Learning from the experts

Some years ago, I had the good fortune to speak with a Tai Chi grandmaster on this subject. Her family has been involved in the martial arts for five generations and her comments were interesting and different from what I'd previously heard from other teachers. Upon reflection, they made the most sense and were comparable with my own experiences.

The grandmaster kindly explained that the mind must be completely quiet when doing the movements of the Tai Chi form, and at first this puzzled me because previously I had been taught that one must have a strong idea about the movement being performed, be it Crane Spreads Wings, Repulse Monkey or Carry Tiger to Mountain, before executing it.

Other teachers from a different lineage had used the saying 'The mind moves the energy and the energy moves the body' to convey the relationship between idea and action, but this is easily open to misinterpretation when trying to absorb Eastern wisdom into English and American culture and language without distinguishing between the analytical mind of the West and the quieter, wider Zen mind of the East.

It's a subtle difference but a crucial one. Intention, not the thinking mind, activates the body's energy, called by various names in different cultures and disciplines, eg Prana (Yoga), Chi (Tai Chi) and Ki (Karate). The energy body in its turn enables physical matter such as the bones, tendons and muscles to fire correctly, in sequence and with minimal effort, sending the ball on its way to the target or allowing a faultless handspring onto the vault.

A clear, simple intention primes the body for the release of even the most complex movement and results in a chain of events which could be summed up in three words: intention, activation and movement. This is an advanced subject and can only be understood or experienced through training, and we'll look at it again a bit later.

Tenpin rehearsal

Bringing this discussion back to the world of sport, here's some interesting feedback on what we might call 'athletic intention' from a friend and mentor I've been working with for many years. Like me, he has pondered on these subjects in depth:

*'When I imagine that I am about to bowl, I am aware
of how I set up to cope with that heavy ball, how
my core and feet trigger the backswing, which also
includes a natural mini squat. There is a tiny pause
before the core and the squat start the follow-through
and release. Lots of power comes naturally out of the
ground and I finish the movements with my weight
having been transferred to my left foot – and I didn't
have to think consciously about any of it. When my
intention is to bowl a heavy ball and I stay with that
without any mental interference, my body knows
what to do. My natural instincts take over and
prepare my intention and then deliver the movement.'*

Intention, rightly accessed from a quiet mind, paves the way for an instinctive set-up or preparation followed by a joined-up, or connected, set of efficient, effective movements.

When the outcome or intention is clear and the focus is held in a relaxed sense of readiness rather than in the self-interfering inner dialogue that wants to get it right, the mind and body can work together (TMB) to recall embedded movement skills without resorting to a mental checklist of instructions.

Any fault that shows up in your movement routine or sequence, whether it's mistiming, lack of tempo, loss of balance or you're way off-target, all begins with a lack of sync between mind and body at set-up. Instead of allowing the body to respond instinctively

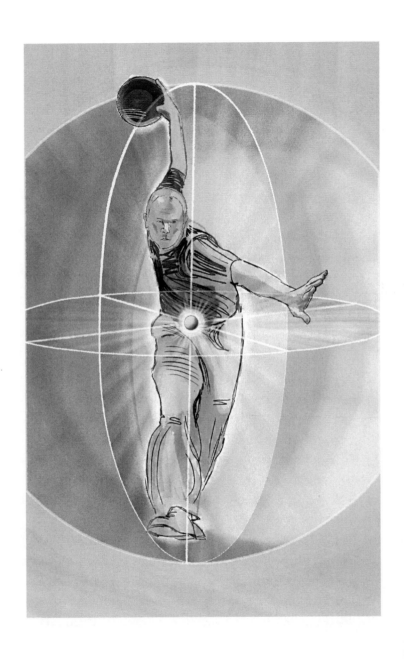

from stillness and intention, your mind gets busy thinking about the movement you're going to perform and goes off into its own little world imagining it can bowl the ball or swing the club or attempt a 360 on the halfpipe.

Simply put, if you don't overthink or try too hard to control your movement skills, especially if they are embedded through repetition and practice, you only need to get out of the way and allow them to be released quite naturally and spontaneously when it matters most. This getting out of your own way cannot be attained through any method, system or formula that gives predominance to the mind, as problems can never be solved on the same level at which they are created.

During a recent podcast interview, the host kept telling me his listeners wanted something 'tangible' to take away from the episode, even though we had spoken for 75 minutes about the role of the quiet mind in delivering a pure golf shot. On reflection, what he was really asking for was a key idea or bullet point, something that the mind can hold on to when trying to get the swing right. This is the myth that needs busting, but it can take many hours or even years of practice before one begins to understand.

Making time each day to sit quietly following your breathing is something real and tangible that has been shown over time to reduce mental chatter and soothe nerves, anxiety and stress. The same cannot be said of psychology or the mental game which still wants you to talk to yourself, however positively and self-affirming it might be, as well as mentally review your technique before executing it.

By now we all know which approach leads to the athlete's ascent and which to their downfall.

Visualisation

Visualisation, or more specifically 'visual motor rehearsal', is another crucial aspect of an athlete's preparation for movement that's been hijacked by the conventional mind-centred approach to sports performance.

Athletes are rightly encouraged to mentally rehearse their shots or routines before performing them. As the mind has trouble distinguishing imagination from reality, the neurons and muscle fibres involved in executing a movement will respond in the same way as in a real-time situation.

One of the most striking examples of this is something I learned from motor racing and shows how specific this form of preparation can be. According to Christopher Hilton, author of *Inside the Mind of the Grand Prix Driver*, if a racing driver visually rehearses a lap of the track and this mental rehearsal takes 1 minute 27.32 seconds, when they get behind the wheel and drive the lap, it takes precisely 1 minute 27.32 seconds to complete.

During a race, however, if the driver thinks rather than responds instinctively from a place of intent, it will delay the signal to the motor system, perhaps only by 1/100th of a second but when the car is approaching a bend at speeds up to 190 miles per hour, even this miniscule delay can be fatal. This is further proof of the crucial distinction between visualisation and analytical thinking.

Any idea or intention you have for your sport must not be too strong or else it engages the prefrontal cortex, whose job is to analyse information. In this case, it will disrupt the signal being sent to the part of the brain that controls movement, throwing off your sequence, timing and reactions. In the above example this could, of course, have disastrous consequences, but in other, less serious, circumstances the results can still be devastating to the athlete if they fail to live up to their own and other people's expectations.

Developing your Performance Practice will help you visualise from a quieter place in yourself, and if you can remember to place some of your attention on your breathing and the body's centre of gravity while visually rehearsing your movements, so much the better. This will ensure you keep some relationship with your body, which stops the prefrontal cortex over-working and calms those feelings of anxiety which can easily turn into CFM.

Sensing the hara

As you progress through this book, you will discover more about the role the physical centre plays in helping the body respond to intention, something that can be explained, for now, using the example of an archer. In this art, called Kyudo in Japanese, preparation for releasing the arrow arises entirely from the hara (later known as the t'an tien in Chinese Kung Fu), which has been termed 'the second brain'.

A quote from one of my favourite books, *Kyudo: The art of zen archery* by Hans Joachim Stein, details the depth of this process and the marked absence of thinking: '*Yugamae means "being prepared" with regard to both inner concentration and the external technical aspects. Mind, body, and technique each presuppose one another, and the quality of one is determined by the quality of the others.*'

Interestingly, the latest research from neuroscientists suggests that it is as important to envision the processes which will lead to a successful outcome as it is to imagine yourself winning the play-off on Sunday afternoon or lifting the trophy as team captain for your local club.

Perhaps this is why the visualisation sequence used by the legendary Jack Nicklaus proved to be so powerful and also why, in my view, part of his strength was in having a quiet mind, void of technical thinking, rather than a tough mind as many others have assumed.

Nicklaus's record of eighteen major golf champion-ships has still not been broken, despite (or maybe because of) all the latest technological breakthroughs in equipment, performance statistics, motion-capture analysis and, of course, the mental game.

Nicklaus would always visualise the outcome first, seeing the ball sitting up high on the fairway. He would then imagine the flight the ball needed to take to land at his chosen spot. Then the picture would change and Nicklaus would imagine sitting on the sofa at home, watching himself on television produc-ing the golf swing required to impact the ball and send it on his chosen trajectory. He would practise like this for each and every shot, whether he was on the range or playing in a tournament.

Visual motor rehearsal

Bringing this approach to your Performance Practice can be extremely powerful, especially if you practise your visualisation skills after quietening your mind in seated meditation. You can also visualise while training yourself to be in a state of relaxed readiness in standing practice or when doing your walking meditation, which we'll look at in Part Two. You can practise two or three times a week, as well as before an event or competition.

Once your mind is quiet, your breathing is deep and slow and your awareness is settled in the t'an tien, spend a few minutes visually rehearsing your desired outcome, whether it's making every hurdle in the upcoming race or slam-dunking with perfect ease while facing down your biggest rival.

You will also want to visualise how you are applying your Performance Practice – at home in the morning, on the way to the competition, track- or courtside and right in the midst of things – all the while being quietly focused within.

The great strength and beauty of this approach is that you will keep to the same practices, whether it's being aware of your posture while sitting on your chair or cushion, listening to your breathing while putting on your kit, holding to your centre when walking out to face the crowd, or feeling your feet on the ground when standing over the ball and enjoying the moment as you deliver your victory speech after the win.

TRY THIS: Making your own success soundtrack

I've been making success soundtracks with my personal clients for years.

Write some notes in your training journal about what you want to achieve in your sport, how your shots and movement routines are going smoothly and how your Performance Practice is helping. You can use the guides to affirmations and visualisation in Part Three of this book to help you.

Once you're ready, record what you've written on your phone with your favourite music playing in the background. Make sure to be supported by an aspect of your Performance Practice, such as holding to your body's centre while recording, which will help foster self-belief and make you sound calm yet confident.

Listen to your soundtrack while training, on the way to competitions, in the locker room etc to reinforce your daily practice and help you remember to apply it in the game.

If you suffer from aphantasia, a rare condition which means you cannot visualise, you can still use meditation to quieten your mind and build power in your affirmations (see Part Three) by focusing on the feelings and sensations you'd experience when achieving your desired goals.

Flow

The flow state and the zone are ways to describe moments of spontaneous excellence when sporting movement, however complex and difficult, simply emerges naturally and often with a feeling that it was somehow without effort. In my view, they represent slightly different aspects, levels or grades on a continuum of consciousness to which the bodymind responds.

We can loosely say that flow is something that occurs in less physical sports like golf, billiards and Archery and that the zone arises during high-energy, reactive sports. Interestingly, it was tennis and baseball stars from the '80s, including the late, great Arthur Ashe, who began referring to a new phenomenon called being in 'the zone', which is now part of common parlance.

In this book, we'll interchange the two terms as we're talking about raising performance for all athletes, and you can relate to whatever resonates and what you'd like to experience in your own sport without getting hung up on terminology.

The most important thing for your purposes is to examine what's happening in the mind, breathing and body of athletes who experience these states in the midst of competition and to focus your energy on learning to recreate the conditions which allow them to manifest. Indeed, the effort needed and the inner conditions required remain the same, and the resultant experiences emerge depending on the athlete and the situation.

In other words, your Performance Practice will focus your energy, attention and much of your training on learning how to prepare the ground and invite flow, or the zone, to appear, allowing your body to respond with graceful, synchronised and spontaneous movement of a markedly different quality from that which can be summoned by mentally reviewing your technique.

Recently I heard a former major winner and world number one golfer lament the fact that it was because he 'wasn't thinking about the present moment' during his last tournament that he was out of contention after day two, having been the favourite to win.

As you develop your Performance Practice, you will avoid this mistake, becoming ever more aware that thinking and being in the moment, just like thinking and following the breath, can never be co-existent. Thinking is always about what has already happened or what is going to happen; it's either about the past or the future, whether that's a tournament three weeks hence or the swing you're intending to perform in a few moments.

Flow can't be attained by thinking but by training the conditions that give rise to it, and in application you just need to allow it to manifest by staying with some aspect of your deep practice and holding a clear but quiet intention.

The holy grail

In sporting movements when no urgency, or indeed reaction, is required, such as a golf shot, a penalty kick, a billiard break or a second serve in tennis, there is plenty of time for the mind to take over and try to organise movement, unless you know how to prevent that from happening and stay quietly connected within.

In reactionary sports, while the athlete is preparing to receive the opposition's ball, the player will instinctively be reading the movements of the server/bowler to interpret their delivery intentions, including the power, direction and flight of the ball, while at the same time planning the shot to play in response.

This can happen in and of itself quite instinctively, but the overarching intelligence of TMB and the natural sequence that occurs as a response to it (intention, activation, movement) will break down if the mind is allowed to dominate.

The greatest athletes in the world know this intuitively and don't allow their mind to get ahead of their movement. For example, in *The 7 Secrets of World Class Athletes*, Steven Yellin and Buddy Biancalana note that Roger Federer, winner of twenty major singles titles, waits longer than any other player on tour before he returns an opponent's shot.

Instead of thinking ahead and pre-empting whether to play an open-stance forehand or run around the ball for a backhand down the line, Federer often wrong-foots his opponent by waiting until the absolute last moment before playing his return shot. This shows unity between mind and body, intent and action, without the mind jumping ahead with ideas of what it wants the body to do.

The perfect shot, high bar dismount or edge jump in figure skating often takes the athlete by surprise, but we're learning to deconstruct, understand and train the conditions within the mind, breathing and body that allow this to happen.

Flow is the elixir, or holy grail, of sporting experience both for the athlete and the spectator, and descriptions of this state range from intensely satisfying to magical and otherworldly.

When you're in flow, everything comes together perfectly, enabling you to perform your shot, technique or routine with grace, power and precision. Body motion is more connected and there is an enhanced fluidity to your movements together with a quiet confidence about your ability to go for the shot or move rather than playing safe.

I'm sure you've had such an experience, only to discover that when you attempted to do the same thing again, in other words when you tried harder on the next shot using technical thinking and psychological methods, it all went horribly wrong or, at least, you weren't able to find the ease of movement you had previously enjoyed. By reading this book, you're already beginning to understand what's happening when mind and movement merge into one and how best to train yourself to enjoy this experience again and again.

Effortless movement is the result of an unmistakable feeling of calm, focus and clarity in the moments before movement begins; these are the conditions of flow that have been relayed to me by hundreds of clients and readers who have all experienced a state which transcends the mind and therefore cannot be trained by thinking. It's a unique combination of being relaxed yet totally alert, resulting in movement that seems to arise of its own accord.

A formula for flow

From LPGA tour players to county-level tennis players, national swimming champions, amateur cyclists and those involved in winter and endurance sports, the feedback I've received about what being in flow feels like describes the following:

- A sense of clarity
- Knowing rather than thinking
- Being in the moment
- Performing evenly and slowly
- Focusing on the target
- Not thinking about technique
- Feeling in the game
- Feeling in the shot
- Trusting

- A sense of calm focus
- Living and playing
- Experiencing deeper enjoyment
- Feeling more confident
- A sense of freedom
- Feeling more relaxed
- Noticing your natural ability comes out
- Feeling your body is in the groove

Popular thought claims that there is a formula for being in the zone, which certainly concurs with my own findings and mirrors what we know about the meditative experience and its benefits to sport.

Flow can be summed up as follows:

Skill + Passion – Mental Interference = Flow

When in a state of flow, the athlete is not distracted by any internal self-talk commenting on the score, technique or personal performance and, moreover, is not disturbed by external factors like their competitors, the weather or noise from spectators. In the meditative state acquired through practices such as awareness of breathing (Zazen) or the physical body (Vipassana), the practitioner is, again, neither distracted by their internal dialogue nor disturbed by external happenings such as noise from the street, children playing outside or the phone ringing.

My own work and research suggests that we can practise getting into flow by developing a routine of daily meditation, but what's often misunderstood is that in meditation practice, as well as sports performance, you can only lay the groundwork in preparation for flow or Zen mind to appear.

You can invite but not force these higher levels to arise by practising again and again to develop a state where your mind, breathing and the initiation of movement are more connected, which then allows entry to these realms of heightened performance. As the great Indian sage and poet Sri Aurobindo reminds us in his book *The Synthesis of Yoga*:

> '*Always indeed it is the higher Power that acts. Our sense of personal effort and aspiration comes from the attempt of the egoistic mind to identify itself in a wrong and imperfect way with the workings of the divine Force.*'

As an interesting aside, the jump shot in basketball and netball is understood to be the most complex and difficult of all sporting movements, with the golf swing coming in a close second. In the jump shot, a player attempts to score a basket by leaping into the air and holding the ball above their head while cocking their lead elbow into position for the shot, sometimes spinning 180 degrees if they're facing away from the basket at the time. In *Tao of the Jump Shot*, John Fitzsimmons Mahoney states that players have more success the less they think about how they are going to make the shot and score more baskets using feeling and instinct, which are classic signs of being in flow.

Natural Movement Principles

Now that we've looked at sports performance from a different perspective than that offered by psychology and the mental game, let's examine centuries-old movement principles that can be applied across all sports and which also show up in everyday life. These can be trained and applied in real-time pressure situations and form the second pillar of your Performance Practice, with seated meditation and breathing being the first.

Some years ago, when I was coaching at a tennis academy for talented youngsters, I picked up an industry magazine to read at lunchtime and found a great article which posited the same principles as I'd been teaching the junior players that morning using movements from the Yang-style Tai Chi form.

The article suggested that squash and tennis players train their legs for increased strength, better balance and quicker, more efficient movement, but they also keep the upper body completely relaxed. The article further claimed that the most effective shots are those where the movements of the upper body follow the rotation of the waist, rather than when the arms move in isolation. The phrase 'Go low and stay loose' stuck in my mind.

In Tai Chi training there's a classic instruction which captures these principles of natural movement and establishes them in their rightful place as the precursor to modern-day biomechanics: *'Rooted in the feet, springing from the legs, moving through the waist, expressed in the hands.'*

This describes the way the body wants to move and does move when it isn't hindered by any form of interference such as nerves, anxiety and the overactive Worry Brain.

When the athlete is under pressure, however, and is trying too hard and thinking too much, this natural order or sequencing (feet, waist, hands) is interrupted as the mind wants to get involved and organise movement, so it's helpful to train these principles with some practices and drills.

Allowing the body freedom

Two things are equally important for enabling the body to move freely and naturally: first, awareness of breathing to quieten the mind and regulate the biochemistry, and second, adhering to fundamental movement principles. We'll look at these more closely now.

When you overanalyse how you're moving or, more precisely, how you're *going* to move in a few moments' time, whether that's diving into the pool, exploding from the starting blocks or preparing for a halfpipe routine, you often get the exact opposite of what you want, as the Worry Brain and the analytical mind kick in, disrupting the signal being sent to the motor system and throwing off your tempo.

Conversely, your ability to perform a flawless technique can be locked down within certain parameters that have nothing to do either with mechanics or the mental game and everything to do with anchoring the attention in the physical body, specifically the four crucial areas of your breathing, posture, centre of gravity, and balance.

These principles harness self-awareness (which, as I once heard tennis legend Billie Jean King say in an interview, is the stuff of champions) and always take priority over technique; they come first and provide the structure within which your technique can operate; indeed, they are the foundations that support your technical skills.

Every shot and every performance is a unique event and cannot be repeated, even if you play the same golf course or repeat the same routine on the same piece of equipment day after day. Fixed patterns of movement decay over time, and if you simply train a set menu of movement positions, something will always need fixing, as anyone who's ever tried to lock down their golf swing will attest to.

This is a phenomenon called Murphy's Law, the principle that if something can go wrong, it will go wrong, which I examine more closely in my book *Breathe Golf*.

If you spend time training natural movement principles (which you're going to start to do in Part Two) alongside the mechanics of your particular sport, they will provide a foundation within which your technique can operate more successfully and be repeated more consistently. These natural movement principles are always rooted in the feet, then they spring from the legs, move through the waist and are expressed in the upper body. They will help you build a relaxed structure so you can deliver your skills effortlessly under pressure.

Looking eastwards to some of history's greatest warriors – from Samurai swordsman and author of *A Book of Five Rings*, Miyamoto Musashi (1584–1645) to Tai Chi, *Xingyi* and Bagua master Sun Lutang (1860–1933) – both of whom would stand motionless for many hours at a time – we see undeniable proof that mastery of stillness does indeed foster mastery of movement.

Rather than practising patterns, ie sword and Kung Fu forms, these fighters honed a unique condition of relaxed readiness where stillness and intention were given priority. This allowed for the release of spontaneous, explosive and devastating motion, whatever was required in the moment, according to the situation, and they were far more effective than any of their opponents.

Trusting the body

As we saw in the tenpin rehearsal, the body understands all about complex movement; it is designed for balance, leverage, torque, rotation and joint stacking and knows far more than your analytical mind does about the kinetic chain and ground forces.

Without the disruptive influence of the mind, your body knows how to call upon these embedded skills, including those from your sport, and execute them in a joined-up way. When the thoughts are subdued and attention is placed on the breathing and the physical centre, TMB is awakened and with it the flow state.

Let's look at the example of a punch rehearsal. When you practise hitting a bag with a fist punch, the intended outcome is delivered without any consideration of individual movements because the intention is clear and the movements happen naturally – you just do it. Of course, your movement can always be trained to be more efficient, but basically a punch is a punch.

The energy of the movement is rooted in the feet and springs up from the ground into the legs; it then passes through the waist and is delivered by the fist, which issues the force that has been transferred from the ground (ideally imagining you are hitting *through* the bag, so you don't decelerate).

When you set up for the punch, you intuitively respond to the intention, be that to deliver a modest tap or a more aggressive attack or indeed a series of blows; the set-up can range from being somewhat casual for the light tap to a solid, almost immoveable base for that more aggressive delivery.

Bruce Lee, although a movie star and Kung Fu giant, was quite a diminutive figure of 5 feet 7 with a body mass index of less than 10% fat, yet he could still knock a man down with a punch issued no further than an inch away from his opponent's body, such was his ability to transfer energy using the proper sequence of movement.

This same sequence or order of movement applies to many everyday activities and instinctive movements, such as throwing a ball or lifting a heavy box off the ground; it can be summarised as the basic principles of Tai Chi and holds true for many of the world's martial arts.

We can see it here in the Aikido image, which shows Aikido founder, Morihei Ueshiba, effortlessly throwing his much younger opponent by staying rooted in the ground and turning through the body's centre – all while maintaining an inner poise and stillness.

It's the same for sports. You can go through the theoretical steps to produce what may look like an orthodox set-up or preparation, but the mind and body will only join together to execute the shot or movement routine effortlessly if the whole process is born of a clear inner intention that is dependent on a quiet mind and a relaxed but ready physical state.

All sports use the same natural, instinctive movements, and your mind and body know how to call upon these movements, plus those that have been rehearsed and ingrained from your particular sport, and release them quite freely and naturally even under pressure, provided you learn to reduce anxiety and stop your mind from interfering.

The sequence from intention through activation to movement can be seen clearly in the above examples and describes the fundamental sequence or natural circuit of effortless motion. Providing it is not interrupted or broken by overthinking or a body that's tight and rigid, the movement will flow unimpeded.

If you notice any signs that you're interrupting this sequence, if you're nervous, anxious or thinking too much, step aside and regroup before taking your shot or performing your routine.

The athlete's role is to lay the groundwork for mind and body to work together without trying too hard to make the perfect shot or perform a flawless routine. A higher level of intense concentration is required, one that is not attached to the result but stays in the moment.

Investing In Loss

We'll finish Part One of *The Athlete's Ascent* with one final word from the martial arts masters of antiquity. 'Investing in loss' is a concept I heard over twenty-five years ago and, like many pearls of Eastern wisdom, it has stayed with me and been a guiding light in my work, life and training ever since. The easiest way of explaining it is to give you an example.

Let's go back to the *Karate Kid* movies where the young, often shy, awkward or disadvantaged boy or girl gets their backside kicked by the older aggressive bully again and again and again to the point where self-doubt, anxiety and emotional upset make them feel they can't go on with their training.

Under the guidance of the wise Mr Miyagi, something subtle but immensely powerful develops: an inner strength and self-belief that has nothing to do with ego and everything to do with the right effort having been made over many weeks, months and years.

Ironically, losing and failing are important steps on your journey. More specifically, overcoming the fear of failure and releasing attachment to the outcome or results of a competition can help you commit to movement in a way that being hesitant or caught up in trying to get it right will never accomplish.

We all know what happens at the end of the film: the bully gets their comeuppance, and the little warrior emerges victorious. In Tai Chi we would say that softness has defeated strength.

Trust the process

Never doubt this new path you're on; the principles and practices you're learning *will* help you triumph in competitive sporting situations no matter if you initially get beaten or nothing seems to be changing. By investing in loss, you're working on something that can't be taken away; it's like putting money in the bank of confidence.

This is not a confidence born from positive self-talk, which has little real substance, but from your innate intelligence and sense of trust that by working to harmonise your mind and body through the medium of your breathing and other deep practices, you are honing a unique inner state that will keep you alert yet relaxed and able to release your movement skills when it matters.

With dedicated and purposeful practice, you can expect to execute your shot or movement routine the way you intend, but at the same time you'll know that if things don't start out as planned, you now have the tools and resources to turn everything around, which gives you multiple advantages over your competitors.

Your Performance Practice brings you the simple, proven and trusted wisdom of the ages specifically applied to your sport in the here and now.

PART TWO
TEN ESSENTIAL PRINCIPLES OF HIGH PERFORMANCE

'Any tension is a loss of awareness; any gain in awareness is an increase in relaxation.'
— Tai Chi Grandmaster Cai Songfang, in Jan Diepersloot, *Warriors of Stillness*

The Principles

I n Part Two, we'll examine what I've discovered to be the Ten Essential Principles of High Performance, before putting them all together into a daily routine in Part Three. Your training here, particularly the standing meditation made famous in more recent years by Wang Xiangzhai and his martial art of *Yiquan* (Intention Fist), together with the *Santi* or Three Levels posture of Sun Lutang's *Xingyi*, will help you build unshakeable parameters within which your sporting skills can be expressed most effectively.

As you've seen, performing under pressure requires a level of self-discipline that goes beyond the usual athletic pursuits of peak fitness, strength and conditioning work, and even technical prowess, although these of course remain vital to your attempts to become the greatest sportsperson you can be.

The new, expanding role for competitive athletes with regards to the emerging paradigm of the mind–body connection encompasses four distinct modes, all of which are necessary for you to significantly raise your performance and enjoyment levels and secure more wins.

These four modes are:

1. Fitness, nutrition, strength and conditioning

2. Technical ability and understanding

3. Developing the state of relaxed readiness with meditation and natural movement principles

4. Keeping your attention in the moment during competition

The strength of your Performance Practice is that it remains the same whether you are sitting in meditation at home, focusing on your breathing as you drive to the golf club, holding your focus in the body's centre as you put on your kit or adopting a relaxed self-awareness, void of analysis and anxiety, as you head out to face the crowd and your opponent.

When you're competing against others, it will rarely be the fittest athlete or the one with more technical know-how who is guaranteed to win but the one who can perform under pressure. As I once heard the youngest ever Wimbledon men's singles champion, Boris Becker, say, *'It's all about who can execute during those big points.'* That means the athlete who can move their body with freedom and deliver fluid yet precise motion when it matters.

To achieve this, your preparation for movement is the all-important factor even though the mainstream rarely assesses the quality of sport by the quality of an athlete's stillness in the moments before motion begins. The research of Dr Fred Travis, which reaffirms the ancient wisdom this training is based upon, shows that this is exactly where you must focus your efforts.

Methods for deep practice

The Ten Essential Principles of High Performance will show you *how* to prepare yourself for movement under pressure by detailing deep practice methods to help unite your mind and body in the moments before you start your routine or take your shot. You are putting much of the mental game, psychology, neuro-linguistic programming and positive thinking to one side (as useful as these things are ahead of the game) and instead concentrating on developing the components that unite intention and action, relaxation and focus, and which allow you to release movement in a way that's free, natural and spontaneous.

Before we examine them in detail, let's take a quick overview of each of the principles and their related practices.

Principle One: Controlling Your Biochemistry. This keystone principle will help you become aware of your breathing using simple but formal meditation to help soothe and calm your nerves and access the relaxation response, enabling your body to move more freely.

Principle Two: Quietening Your Mind. This is a foundational principle which you can develop by working with your breathing to help quieten down your thinking processes, especially those of the Worry Brain or analytical mind.

Principle Three: Holding the Centre. This principle is another cornerstone which helps garner the attention in your body's physical centre of gravity, from where you can learn to initiate relaxed yet powerful movement, especially centrifugal force.

Principle Four: Relaxed Readiness. In this principle you'll look at the inner conditions which allow entry to the experience of flow and how you can train for this state and apply it pre-shot or pre-routine using various deep practices such as seated, standing and walking meditation.

Principle Five: Listening. This principle explores the Tai Chi concept of listening to the body to gather crucial biofeedback about your current internal state. This will enable you to feel the signs and symptoms of anxiety and stage fright so you can nullify them before you strike the ball or begin your dismount.

Principle Six: Self-observation. In this principle you'll be learning how to access the observer mind, which, in addition to the sensory data you'll be gathering through listening, will help you to see the effects nerves, anxiety and mental interference are having on your preparation and free yourself of them before commencing your movement skills.

Principle Seven: Making Time. Here you'll learn why it's important to take your time so that the conditions of flow have a chance to manifest *before* you attempt to perform any complex movement. When you rush your preparation, you disrupt any chance of getting in flow, so in this principle you'll be learning how to slow down.

Principle Eight: Just Enough. This is another useful concept from Tai Chi, which can help you bring just the right amount of energy and just the right amount of attention to the task you're about to perform without wasting these vital resources in worrying, overthinking or being anxious.

Principle Nine: Wonder and Awe. In this principle you're going to take a step back and look at how the extraordinary experience of flow, so akin to the meditative state, is really just that, *extra*-ordinary – it's beyond our understanding and certainly beyond our control, although it is possible to develop the ability to access this state more often.

Principle Ten: Downtime and Recuperation. In this final principle you're going to take a break and allow yourself time for some much-needed reflection. As with everything else in life, a practice such as meditation can easily become a habit. To keep it real, you'll need to step away now and then so you can regroup and process the changes that are taking place within you, and particularly how they're showing up in your sport.

Try to read all the way through the Ten Principles before you start your practice and keep notes in your training journal about the things that seem most relevant to your situation as it is now; in other words, take what you want from this programme that can immediately help you perform better in pressure situations. There is no special order in which you need to practise, just start with what appeals and seems most pertinent.

Make sure you write in a journal or notebook rather than jotting things down on your phone or tablet. University studies have consistently shown that the physical act of writing enhances neurological processes in the brain, which can improve your concentration. Conversely, the more time you spend on your devices, the shorter your attention span becomes, and, as you're beginning to realise, what you do with your attention is crucial to being able to perform under pressure.

Principle One: Controlling Your Biochemistry

The golf swing, tennis serve, penalty kick, back-flip and free throw are all complex movements which must be learned and honed by developing good hand–eye co-ordination and a correct technique, plus committing to the inevitable practice and repetition.

Once you've learned the skills, you would think that the movements would become automatic and you wouldn't have any trouble executing them in competition, but, as we all know, things aren't as easy as that, otherwise everyone who enjoys sport would be a world-class superstar.

The problem is that complex movement is just that... complex. As we've seen, thinking and worrying about how to perform the movement correctly just gets in the way of moving freely, powerfully and naturally.

Without developing a Performance Practice, the list of how the pressure-induced stress response limits your ability to express movement includes a whole range of debilitating symptoms that stop you executing your skills well. Your muscles shorten and tighten, there is less oxygen being sent to the brain, your adrenaline levels and heart rate increase, and everything that affects the fluidity of motion, like losing your balance or timing, comes to the fore.

There is, however, one fundamental activity, something you're doing right now, that can alleviate all these factors and help restore calm and equilibrium so you can play the shot you want or be brave enough to go for the 360-degree flip you usually avoid.

As human beings, we have the astonishing ability to regulate our breathing, and when we learn to do this in a pressure situation, we also regulate our biochemistry, which in turn enables the use of our movement skills. Of course, it is simple in principle but requires a dedicated practice to apply it, as most of the time we remember neither our breath nor our body but live in the mind's constructions of past and future.

Your Performance Practice becomes the vital link between each principle and having it show up in a real-time competitive situation. Without it, you'll stay in the mainstream world of thinking about thinking and thinking about moving.

What's amazing is that when you start this work, the difference between the stress response and relaxation response will be so keenly felt that you'll develop the ability to recognise the symptoms of stress as they arise and learn to monitor your own brain–body chemistry according to the situation.

Here's how a client explained what it felt like to finally play to his potential on the golf course, having stuck with his practice over several weeks:

> *'Dear Jayne. Since starting with you I played and won my first match today, beating my opponent by one hole with a birdie at the eighteenth! What it comes down to is I simply do your meditation exercises to my best ability and then just let it happen on the course. So, I am trusting my mind and body together to work it out for me. That's the best way I can explain the seismic shift that I am experiencing. It really has been a shock to suddenly strike the ball such distance and to find I am on the green in regulation! You really have thought all this out very carefully from the drills to the applications and they all work beautifully. Thank you.'*
> – Christopher S

When I was researching and developing my approach, I came across many scientific papers and books about flow and the phenomena of being in the zone, but unfortunately most of the studies available are written from a psychological perspective, which, from my extensive experience, seems to somehow miss the point.

Psychology is useful in that it can help to examine, deconstruct and reorganise our everyday thought processes, but the flow state, or zone, is *beyond* the ordinary level of the mind; it takes the individual experiencing it into the realm of Zen mind, or no mind, where the prefrontal cortex, which is usually busy thinking and analysing, goes offline, leaving the mind free, open and spacious.

Psychology can take you to the doorway, but it will not let you into the real experience of flow, the benchmark of which is the Eastern approach to mind–body unity and the various practices, like awareness of breathing, which have been used for centuries to attain this.

The six areas of the brain

To further demonstrate the efficacy of a regular meditation practice, let's examine the various centres and regions of the brain and show which ones are necessary for you to perform effortless movement under pressure and which ones hinder this, making it difficult, if not impossible, for you to move well when you need to. We'll also look at how the way you breathe can influence these centres.

The brain is a complicated clump of interconnected nerve cells. These are organised in clusters, or brain centres, each of which has a different role. For instance, there are separate and specific centres for moving a limb, hearing, remembering, speaking and so on.

For a better understanding of how meditation practice works, it can be helpful to divide the brain into six different areas. These are: Thinking Brain, Motor Brain, Worry Brain, Calming Brain, Breathing Brain and the Spinal Column.

The **Thinking Brain** analyses different options for the shot you want to play or the movement routine you're about to perform. It then decides which golf club to use or where in the goal you want your penalty kick to land. It then orders the Motor Brain to execute the shot.

The **Motor Brain** has several good shots and routines in its archives – the ones you've performed effortlessly on the driving range or during practice with your teammates. It will execute these moves faultlessly unless it is disturbed by influences from the Worry Brain, in which case it will activate an alternative sequence, which then leads to an errant golf shot or a poor kick that hits the post.

These 'default' moves show up every time you start overthinking and lose the connection to your breathing and your physical centre. We'll talk more about this later.

What's interesting is that in golf, for instance, every player will have a preprogrammed good swing and bad swing. The bad swing will invariably show up at least one of the most common swing faults when the connection to the Motor Brain is disrupted; for example, shortening the backswing and decelerating through impact or not following through, which swing coaches try resolving through mechanical coaching.

When the mind is quiet, the better, more fluid swing will usually manifest itself, as the body is able to move freely and according to the natural movement principles it fully understands. Let's consider what happens in these brain centres during a good golf shot. The same, of course, applies to any sporting movement.

The Thinking Brain decides what shot to make and instructs the Motor Brain to execute that shot. The right club will have been chosen and crucial procedures for executing the shot will have been used, including a number of deep abdominal breaths into the body's centre of gravity and awareness of physical sensations, like the weight of the body and its connection to the ground. This will activate the

Calming Brain and with it the flow state. This vital preparation should not take more than 10–12 seconds and can include a visual motor rehearsal of the planned shot.

The **Worry Brain** is a simplified name for the prefrontal cortex, which is like the CEO of the brain who gets overexcited and wants to micromanage everything, including complex movement, which clearly isn't its job. Its role is to scan for risks, dangers and unsatisfactory outcomes. It is a dominant part of the brain and is important for survival but activating this part of the brain prior to movement results in mistiming, a broken kinetic chain, a clumsy shot, lack of rhythm and all the signs of poor form.

The **Calming Brain** is also known as the occipital cortex. When this region of the brain is activated, it soothes you and will calm things down, reducing anxiety and quietening the thought processes. In electrical recordings of the brain, this region is shown to produce alpha waves, which show up when the mind is in the state of flow or when practising breathing meditation. Interestingly, they don't show up when listening to a mindfulness app on your smartphone.

The **Breathing Brain** is fundamental to your survival. It is sensitive to oxygen and carbon dioxide and drives the muscles associated with breathing, of which there are two main types:

1. Quick, shallow breathing which engages the chest muscles is activated in emergency situations; it's the fight-flight-freeze response which can help to save our lives but is disastrous for performing in high-pressure sports. Without the understanding and awareness gained from a daily meditation practice, many coaches advise their athletes to take a deep breath or even several deep breaths before exiting the gates at the top of a ski run or executing a tennis serve, but this is often counterproductive, as the breathing tends to be in the chest, causing more anxiety.

2. Deep abdominal breathing is associated with tranquillity and inner calm and is ideal for performing complex movement in a way that is fluid, connected and effortless. This is the breathing you'll be practising and honing so it can have the most beneficial influence on releasing your movement skills.

The **Spinal Column** is simply the channel for the nerve impulses to travel from the brain, in the right sequence, to the various muscles involved in either a connected or a disconnected movement – a good golf swing or a bad golf swing, a fluid backhand return or one that lands outside the baseline.

A fundamental aspect of your Performance Practice will be to help you link the Breathing Brain to the Calming Brain so you can perform your movements naturally in pressure situations. By practising the different exercises you're learning in this programme, it is possible to achieve the intentional stillness which meditators and martial artists have long described as the 'master of motion'.

The unique feature of Chi Performance is that it does away with psychological and mental game interventions and instead provides a simple, proven and workable method to activate the Calming Brain, therefore increasing your chance of entering flow.

TRY THIS: Breathing focus

Choose an activity related to your sport where you will try and remember to focus on your breathing. It could be anything from lacing up your trainers to putting on your golf glove or strapping on your skis.

Do this not only in competition but also whenever you're practising, working out in the gym or even just putting your kit in the wash. Anything that's related to your sport can become a useful reminder of your breathing.

Seated meditation

Let's begin your Performance Practice now with this guide to seated meditation.

Schedule at least three sessions of 15–20 minutes each in your weekly planner when you know you're

not going to be disturbed. Try to commit to these times and to the promise you've made to yourself when the appointments come around. Meditating first thing in the morning seems to work best for most people, so you can get your practice out of the way before the day begins, even if you have to get up a bit earlier.

Making this additional effort will be a valuable way to help prepare yourself to come back to your breathing again and again at work, play, driving the car or carrying the groceries. If you can do this, you are far more likely to remember your breathing and bring the full focus of your attention to it to restore calm and inner quiet ahead of your next competition.

There are three ways you can choose to sit, all of which are traditionally used in various Eastern disciplines:

1. **Cross-legged on the floor with your hands at the navel:** Put a couple of cushions or a bolster underneath you (making sure your hips are higher than your knees) and aim to form a half-lotus position with one foot on the opposite thigh. If this is too difficult, just have your feet and lower legs on the ground parallel to each other without trying to cross them – a method practised in Korea which I find the most comfortable.

   Once you are settled, lift up the back of your head and pull your chin in. Cup your hands one palm inside the other and place them slightly below the navel, on the t'an tien. Lower your eyelids until they are almost closed and breathe naturally in and out through your nose.

2. **Kneeling back on your heels (as practised in many Karate schools):** Place your weight back on your heels and maintain an upright posture with your hands cupped in your lap or palms facing down, resting on your thighs. If it's more comfortable, you can place a cushion underneath your backside.

   The back of your head is pushed upwards and your chest and diaphragm push gently down-wards to add strength to your posture and maintain balance physically and mentally. You can sit with your eyelids lowered or look straight ahead at a blank wall.

3. **Upright in a chair with your feet on the floor (as taught in certain Tai Chi lineages):** Keep your spine straight and imagine your head is suspended by a thread from above. Notice the sensation of your feet on the floor. (Have you remembered to try this again?) Press one palm to your navel and cup the other palm over the back of this hand. Lower your eyelids without closing them completely and, as with the other two posi-tions, breathe quietly and smoothly through the nostrils.

The most important thing, whichever option you choose, is to keep a good posture with your head upright and your spine straight while retaining some strength in your lower abdomen. You also want to relax as much as possible but without losing the posture. In each of the positions, try to maintain a simple awareness of your body, breathing and the lower part of your abdomen. Don't try too hard but notice when your mind starts wandering and gently bring your attention back within yourself and continue to follow your breathing.

Principle Two:
Quietening Your Mind

The simplest training, consistently applied, can help you transform your inner state in the moments before you start moving through your shot or routine and alleviate much of the anxiety associated with performance.

Over time you may notice the symbiotic relationship between your breathing, your mind and your body when practising meditation. When the breathing deepens and slows down, your mind will be much quieter and your body will feel alive and alert, but you might also see how all too soon your attention wanders and an effort is required to return to the breath each time you get distracted.

Why apps aren't enough

Mindfulness apps are used by millions of people and have even been given to Team GB athletes as part of their preparation for world-class competitions such as the Olympics. Apps are all well and good as a starting point, and many students have commented that listening to a guided meditation on their smartphone kick-started their journey into more formal practice, but little effort is required to listen and follow along and as a result little change can occur in the individual.

When using an app, nothing is required of the user and moments of flow might appear by chance; yet when you make the effort yourself, a deeper attention is called for so that your experience of flow no longer remains an accident but something that you intend or invite by your practice. Apps are a passive rather than active approach and don't suit the work ethic associated with those who love sport, who are, on the whole, disciplined and used to gruelling training regimes.

I was speaking with a group of my golf clients recently who have each been consistent with their breathing meditation, sitting quietly once or twice each day for several months or years. Many of them said that it is *because* of their formal practice that they are able to come close to being in the body and the breathing when standing over the ball.

Granted, this isn't what you want to hear; you might wish to believe the faddish trend that sees mindfulness as a psychological approach which entails focusing the mind to achieve success and peak performance. It sounds good, but it's a trap you mustn't fall into.

As one PGA pro said to me recently, *'I see my Performance Practice as payment for playing great golf.'* The effort you make is the price you pay for enjoying the flow state more often and there is no way around this no matter what YouTube commentators or social media influencers will have you believe.

You would be better advised to listen to wisdom from Sri Aurobindo, who wrote, *'There is no other way than to persevere,'* or Gurdjieff, who said that without great personal effort nothing of any value can be attained, or the Zen Buddhists who ask us 'under all circumstances' to continue watching the breath.

Being in the present moment standing over your tee shot or tossing the ball ready for your second serve has nothing to do with thinking, not even positive thinking or reframing negative associations; it's about being fully there, in your body, in your breathing, which isn't at all easy but is possible through aspiration and inner struggle.

A new student had this immediate insight after changing from using a mindfulness app to starting a more formal practice: *'How can I be anywhere but in the present if I am engaged with the breath I'm taking now?'*

If you're a competitive athlete who's tried every which way to perform your best under pressure, only to have nerves, anxiety and mental interference hinder your freedom of movement, this is the path you now need to take.

Breathing into the moment

In competition, when the nervous system is aroused, the stress response is induced and the Worry Brain gets overactive, then all the negative thought chains and associations come flooding back into the mind, disrupting the fragile connection to the body, taking you away from the now.

The more you've attempted to bring your attention back to your breathing again and again in your practice and in everyday life, the more able you will be to do this when you really need to.

In a pressure situation, you're going to receive a lot of biofeedback, which shows up in different ways for different people; these are signs and signals that you're out of sync, you're rushing, your mind is racing, and you need to settle down and collect yourself before taking your shot or starting your movement routine. We'll look at this more closely in Principle Five: Listening.

As you bring your attention to your breathing in such moments, all the noise in your head quietens down and space is created in the midst of the mental chatter, a space to be still, a pause to get centred, a gap for flow to manifest as you prepare to receive the pitch or get ready to begin your gymnastics floor routine.

The transformation that occurs when you breathe into the moment is astounding. It puts a halt to all the thinking about past mistakes or let-downs and all the projections about what might happen in the future. This is something you'll want to practise more and more as the day of your competition draws near.

For many athletes, performance anxiety can begin anywhere up to three weeks before the tournament or event; it wreaks havoc with eating and sleeping patterns, it can affect your relationships with family, friends and teammates, and it invokes a variety of imaginary scenarios you may find yourself fretting over rather than spending time deepening your practice.

Some years ago, I was working with a masters-level swimmer, helping her to bring her breathing and intention together poolside before big races, as she was friendly with one of the other competitors and felt badly for her every time she won and her friend lost.

Over the course of her training, my client became focused on only her breathing and began winning medal after medal as she stopped wasting energy worrying about her friend and began swimming without mental or emotional distractions slowing her down.

Your focus from now on is not just to practise technique and train in the gym, important though these things are, but to quietly witness your breathing, following the inhalation and exhalation of air – the purest, simplest and most fundamental of all your activities. You should begin to do this not just when you sit in meditation but whenever you remember and whenever you're doing something connected to your sport so that there is no room for any type of mental interference or emotional negativity to disturb your preparation or performance.

TRY THIS: Preparing for a competition

Use short bursts of meditation (ie a few deep breaths) any time you feel anxious about performing, even if it's weeks before the competition. As the day of the event draws closer, use these short bursts as often as you remember; for instance, when driving to the golf club, sitting in the locker room, hearing the spectators cheer for your opponent or when you walk out onto the pitch.

Any moment when you remember to breathe and hold still for a short pause is a form of attention training and conditioning that will help you to perform 'in the moment' without anxiety or mental interference.

Remember the components of intention which we looked at earlier: a highly focused form of attention directed towards the required outcome minus any investment in the results. When you're truly in the moment, there are no thoughts of winning or losing, no consideration of your competitors, sponsors or the crowd, just a simple joy at moving your body with ease.

Your Performance Practice is for one thing only: to awaken the inner presence in meditation and come back to it moment after moment in your everyday life; then you'll have a better chance of experiencing this instead of feeling anxious, nervous and telling yourself all the reasons why you won't make the shot.

What you're going to discover is that the *only* way to prepare yourself for the upcoming tournament or competition is to practise being in the moment you're in now. This holds true for everyone, to wit, my personal story about demonstrating Tai Chi in front of highly experienced teachers.

This is the secret to delivering effortless motion in high-pressure situations and you can begin to develop a seamless thread between every aspect of your preparation and performance by remembering your breathing, quietening your mind and inhabiting your body in a way that's alert yet relaxed as often as you remember.

I've spent my lifetime practising Tai Chi and other martial arts from China and more latterly India, where the emphasis is on finding a unique quality that includes both focus *and* relaxation, an experience that arises when you're in flow. To this endeavour a huge part of the training is about holding the mind at a specific location within the body, and this is what we're going to take a look at now.

Principle Three:
Holding The Centre

Much of this programme presents traditional Eastern wisdom, which has been verified over the past few decades by Western sports science and neuroscience. We're now touching on a unique aspect of the martial and Zen arts, which is an integral part of mind–body disciplines from Archery to Zazen.

Nothing like it exists in mainstream models of the athletic body or biomechanics, and yet in the Eastern world the lower t'an tien, or hara centre, is considered as the 'second brain', the source of life, the residing place of the breath, a natural centre for the attention and, perhaps most incredibly of all, the initiation point of movement.

It's a big topic but we're going to take a brief look at three main ways you can develop awareness of the t'an tien in your Performance Practice plus some simple applications to best engage this area when you're competing and under pressure.

Working with the t'an tien

First, we need to locate this vital centre. It's roughly 2.5 inches below the navel and two-thirds of the way towards the spine. I encourage my clients to think of this area like a golf or tennis ball that works as a pivot or fulcrum of movement around which the upper body can rotate *without* disturbing the stability of the legs.

Every athlete knows about the importance of core strength, but the t'an tien is like the core's core, the Chi core if you like, and is one of the body's centres of energy and power.

In ball sports, the hands holding the club, bat or racket are generally in line with the t'an tien at set-up and impact, and in other sports like figure skating or gymnastics, when this area is employed the speed and precision of rotational movements are greatly enhanced. If you spin, rotate or recoil in any of your sporting movements, you'll want to get in touch with your t'an tien; perhaps you've even felt its influence at times when everything flowed.

Attention

'Keep your mind within yourself' is a classic instruction from Tai Chi training. Once you develop your daily meditation practice, you might begin to notice how few are the moments in the day when the mind and body come together. It's usually just the opposite, as the mind tends to dominate, either ruminating on past events, similar to a cow chewing the cud, or leaping forward into the future, imagining all kinds of scenarios. To help keep the attention within the body, it's useful to let the mind rest at this vital centre.

As with all aspects of your Performance Practice, it's helpful not to be too serious or earnest about it, otherwise you can end up trying too hard and thinking too much about your breathing, which of course will have the opposite effect to what is desired. Instead, aim to bring a state of relaxed focus to your meditation and to those times during the day and when playing your sport when you want to follow your breathing, be in your centre or feel your feet on the ground. You'll find that as the mind rests in the t'an tien, the shoulders, chest and waist also relax, which is one of the great benefits of mind–body training over psychology and technical thinking alone.

Breathing

Once your mind is settled in the t'an tien, you'll find that your breathing also seems somehow to be connected to this area. To aid this, when you exhale imagine pushing some of the air down to the lower abdomen. Don't use force but rather the idea of creating a stronger Chi core by storing the goodness you've extracted from the breath in your centre.

Many of my clients have reported that this practice fills them with a calm inner confidence and helps to stabilise the emotions. Using the t'an tien as an anchor point for your breathing also stops the mind wandering and worrying and allows the body to respond naturally to the mind's intention, as in the *Yugamae* preparation in Archery shown in the image above.

Movement

Using the t'an tien as a pivot around which the upper body can rotate creates an incredible amount of speed and power, which can penetrate right through a golf, tennis or baseball in your swing and strikes. It also helps to transfer forces generated in the ground and lower body through the waist and into the dominant arm, for instance, when bowling.

The principles of natural movement must include the resolution of opposing forces, as the upper body is soft and yielding and the lower body is rooted and firm and holds the structural stability of the posture.

Spinning or rotating through the body's centre offers this resolution and brings a sense of freedom to the upper body, allowing for more efficient movement through the kinetic chain. It's only by relaxing the upper body that the energy from the legs can be transferred into the arms. If you've experienced this, you'll know it's far more powerful than trying to muscle through the shot with the arms alone.

TRY THIS: Empty-hand drills

Practise empty-hand drills using the t'an tien to initiate the movement of the golf swing, tennis serve or baseball strike. You will need to be balanced and feel strong in your legs while letting the upper body relax. Concentrating on the navel area helps to resolve these opposites, which are the most effective way of transferring vertical force.

After a few minutes, repeat the drill using your club, racket or bat, and finish by doing the drill as you hit some balls.

Hold on to your centre while going through any preparations for your sport; for instance, when you're settling into the starting blocks, standing poolside before a race or about to perform a difficult trick on the halfpipe.

What happens to your shoulders, chest and breathing when you do this; what happens to your mind? Make a note in your training journal.

Your Performance Practice is all about connection, which must be trained: the connection of the mind to the body, of the breathing to the centre, and of the attention to the moment you're in.

In the East, this connection is trained sequentially: first in stillness, then in simple, natural movements like walking, often done in slow motion, before more explosive actions like kicks and punches, which are developed through the repetition of forms and katas. In a fight situation, the inner stillness is retained, and the enlightened warrior responds with whatever move is appropriate at the time.

Bring this into your sports training by holding your ready position – over the golf ball, standing on the baseline, or in the penalty area – anchoring your breathing and your awareness in the t'an tien without letting thoughts or emotions disturb your focus. This will be useful for those high-pressure moments, which are usually when nerves, adrenaline and mental interference cause a widening of the mind–body split, activating both the stress response and the Worry Brain.

When the mind–body split is exacerbated, there is also a more pronounced disconnection of the upper body from the lower body and a raising of the centre of gravity from the lower abdomen into the chest, throwing off your balance, timing and accuracy. Conversely, when your mind and breathing reside in the t'an tien, you will be closer to the inner stillness that always precedes effortless movement.

Principle Four:
Relaxed Readiness

So far, we've been exploring how the mind can either interfere with or positively influence the release of natural movement. We've established that when you overthink, particularly in terms of so-called positive thinking, or when you have too many technical thoughts as you're about to take your shot or start your routine, it interferes with the delicate balance of the mind–body connection.

When the mind takes over and tries to control the way the body moves, instead of a sweet ball strike or a fluid, balanced dismount, you'll find that your timing is off, you're hesitant and things don't flow the way they can when you get out of your own way.

What's interesting about all this is that the mind and body work best together when you're thinking as little as possible. When you're in a more Zen-like state as the thoughts move to the back of the brain, specifically the occipital lobe, a unique and quite extraordinary state of relaxed attention or relaxed concentration becomes possible.

This state, which we know in sport as the zone, or flow, is midway between trying and not trying, thinking and not thinking; it's distinct and makes all the difference between a serve that catches the line and one that goes into the net.

It's exactly the same with the body. When we examine the physical state of athletes in the moments before they explode from the blocks at the start of a 200-metre race, or drive the ball 250 yards off the tee, similar conditions exist as they do with the mind.

As the optimum performance state for the mind is quiet yet concentrated, so it is with the body. When the body is athletic but relaxed, when it has good structure, yet this structure is pliable rather than being stiff or rigid, it allows for movement that is powerful yet controlled, fluid yet precise.

Where can you find the training for this? It certainly isn't in the gym or in mainstream biomechanics, which are more concerned with muscular strength and the force or potential energy that can be generated from the physical body allied with mental toughness.

Looking again to the martial arts of the East, you will find exactly the right exercises to help you develop a physical structure that is strong but flexible and which can allow you to *work with* natural forces like balance, gravity and spin, without trying too hard to create these forces yourself. The latter approach only leads to injury and frustration, as the harder your mind tries, the worse your body moves. The ideal physical posture, called *sung* in Tai Chi, which literally translates as relaxed power, is a big subject and is explored in depth in my book *Connected Golf*.

Let's do some of this training now before we try to understand more about its possibilities for helping you master those pressure situations.

Standing meditation (*Yiquan*)

There are many ways to practise standing meditation, which is the foundational practice of all the internal martial arts. It was popularised in the 1920s by Wang Xiangzhai but its roots go back through time to the warriors of antiquity. Later styles, such as Karate, also have standing postures (for example, the horse stance) but the emphasis of the training is often on building up external (physical) rather than internal (intrinsic) strength.

As with your seated meditation, your posture for standing practice is all-important; your spine should be straight and your head lifted upwards so that you are not slumped or tilted, and you should have a strong sense of inhabiting your physical body. Again, try to put some strength in your lower abdomen, similar to when you have to steel yourself with courage and determination facing a difficult situation. For our purposes, you can choose to stand in one of three ways.

1. **Stand like a monk:** When standing like a monk, your heels should be as far apart as the width of your own fist with your toes pointing forwards. Make a loose fist with your left hand and hold it against your sternum with your thumb and forefinger uppermost. The thumb should be on the outside of the fingers. Now rest your right palm over the top of your left thumb, keeping both hands gently pressed towards the chest. Keeping your forearms parallel to the floor, notice how the left hand pushes up while the right hand pushes down, making a strong and stable posture. Gently look into the distance while maintaining awareness of your breathing.

2. **Stand like a tree:** When standing like a post or tree (*Zhan Zhuang*) your feet should be a little wider than your shoulders with the toes pointing slightly outwards and your weight evenly distributed. Your arms are raised up at shoulder-height, forming a circle with your palms facing inwards towards you as if you're

holding the trunk of a large tree. Keep your spine straight and hold your head as if it's suspended by a thread from above. Your knees should be soft but not bent and your eyes look straight ahead. Maintain awareness of your body's centre and let the breath settle into this area.

3. **Stand like a warrior:** When standing like a warrior (*Santi* or Three Levels posture), you will have one foot in front of the other (as when stepping), a little narrower than shoulder-width, with 80% of your weight resting on your back leg and 20% of your weight on your front leg. Your arms should be engaged in a guarding position down the centre line of your body, with the shoulders, chest and elbows relaxed. Aim to find the perfect position – you should feel as if you're about to spring forwards to attack your opponent. In this classic posture from Chinese Kung Fu, demonstrated in the image below, your arms will match your legs so that if your right leg is to the rear, your right palm presses to the floor at navel height with the left arm extended over the left leg, palm facing forwards. This is the most challenging of all three postures and you may find you can only hold it for a few minutes before switching sides, bringing the opposite leg to the front etc.

With each posture, try to maintain a subtle state between tension and relaxation so that your body is alert, lively and dynamic with a strong but elastic posture. Let your mind rest at the t'an tien and keep your breathing deep, slow and quiet. You must concentrate within but outwardly look relaxed.

Aim to stand for 10–15 minutes each session, and don't be surprised if it takes you several weeks to build up to this – the training is much harder than you think. Try to practise two or three times per week, alternating it with your seated meditation.

The wisdom of Kung Fu

The Cantonese word *sung* denotes a unique and specific quality that combines structure with relaxation. It can only be trained with exercises such as the various standing postures described above, which originated in the Shaolin Temple in 495 CE when Yoga and the Indian martial art of Kalaripayattu, which is 3,000–5,000 years old, met with Chinese culture to become Chi Kung and later Kung Fu.

The training is subtle yet powerful and has been developed by successive generations of families and schools working on particular and exacting principles, many of which are unheard of and certainly not taught in Western sports science. You'll find lots of articles, blog posts, diagrams, podcasts and videos on my website to help you with the postures. Just visit www.chi-performance.com.

According to Kung Fu wisdom, it's the combination of structure plus relaxation that produces the most power, and it is the differing qualities of the upper body and lower body that creates greater speed and precision.

What you're looking to develop with the standing practice is a correct skeletal structure where your joints are stacked one on top of the other – shoulders, hips, knees and ankles – and where the rear of your body is straight with your head lifted upwards while the front of your body is soft with the chest and waist sinking down.

You'll find that this training creates a particular sensation in the body: it's switched on, primed and activated for movement while still relaxed. It might be helpful to think of a tiger or a snake, both of which are always poised and ready to pounce on their prey while seemingly half-asleep. You'll feel alert and ready while your mind, breathing and energy will reside gently in the centre of gravity and the lower part of the body, including the feet.

It's a different experience to be engaged like this with the physical sensations of the body rather than worrying about how you're going to perform or whether you're going to get your technique right. You're switching your body into a state of preparedness for spontaneous rather than rehearsed movement.

When we relax according to conventional Western wisdom, we are taught to relax completely, but while this might be nice if you're curled up watching a movie, it isn't going to help you master pressure. Conversely, if we put too much emphasis on structure and the positions of the body without incorporating the feeling of *sung*, the body tends towards stiffness and the centre of gravity rises to the chest along with the breathing, creating all sorts of problems with movement.

It might help to think of a perfectly tensioned bow: it's not too slack and it's not too tight and this is echoed in the condition of the archer's body, which is poised like the arrow, full of potential energy waiting to be released.

The standing practice exercises will give you a feeling of grounding and support in your feet when you're standing over the ball or waiting to strike on the pitch, but instead of worrying about your upcoming shot, you will feel relaxed and ready to execute your skills.

In addition to standing meditation, ancient wisdom promotes the deep practice of moving in slow motion – as in Tai Chi. Champion athletes from many sports have also employed the slow-motion approach in training sessions, most notably Ben Hogan in golf, Jonny Wilkinson in rugby and Monica Seles in tennis.

Before we look more closely at sport-specific slow-motion practice, let's get you started on the traditional practice of slow walking, which is usually done between long bouts of seated meditation in the monasteries of Japan and after standing practice in the Kung Fu temples of China. You can choose to walk in a straight line, a circle or a figure of eight.

Slow-walking meditation

Walking meditation (Kinhin) serves several purposes, not least of which is to keep the mind within the body, operating at the same speed as physical movement rather than getting ahead of where you are and what you're doing.

This default separation of the mind and body, which can occur during any physical activity, was again made clear to me one day towards the end of a long bike ride. As I turned into my road, I still had a few minutes to cycle before I made it home, but I saw vividly how my mind leapt out of my body. I started imagining that I was sitting at my office desk answering emails and doing other admin jobs that I had to tackle when I got back. Yet I was still on my bike.

Other benefits of this practice include the deepening of your self-awareness and the ability to observe movement in minute detail so that you can refine and hone your skills.

Begin in any of the postures described in the standing meditation exercises and let your mind settle into the soles of your feet. To aid this, relax your chest and feel the weight of your upper body pressing downwards. As you begin to walk, lift one foot and feel the whole weight of your body settle into the foot remaining on the ground.

Move as slowly as you can, allowing your weight to shift completely from the rear foot into the foot you are about to place on the floor. This seems easy, but challenge yourself to slow it down and maintain all the key points of good posture, such as the eyes looking forwards, the head held upright and the chest remaining empty.

As you continue, try to inhale as you lift each foot off the ground, and notice a slight feeling of buoyancy as your lungs fill. As you exhale and place your foot down, relax all the joints and tendons in the body and let any tension sink down through the leg and into the sole of the foot.

Aim to practise for 5–10 minutes several times per week, and mix and match your various Performance Practices according to what you enjoy and what you feel you need. You'll find this exercise in particular will help to calm your nerves and keep you in the moment as you walk down the fairway to your next shot or walk behind the baseline to receive your opponent's serve.

Slow-motion practice

As with most Eastern practices that were once thought of as a bit left field, moving in slow motion has now been proven by neuroscience to have specific benefits due to its particular effects on the brain and the mind–body connection. As explained in *The Harvard Medical School Guide to Tai Chi*, by Peter M Wayne, the neural connections associated with movement are known to get stronger as more detailed and refined information becomes available to the brain to build the movement map.

The following drills are used by my personal clients, and once you understand the principles, they can easily be transferred to any sport.

By slowing down, you can sense differences in muscular effort, which increases your brain's ability to correct any postural and movement imbalances. Your proprioceptive map – the physical areas of your brain responsible for sensing and controlling movement – develops stronger neural linkages in response to slow-motion activity and the resulting sensory feedback that occurs.

Let's look at the slow-motion practice drills for golf and tennis, and remember, the principles apply to any and all forms of complex sporting motion, so don't be afraid to experiment.

THE SLOW-MOTION SWING DRILL

Set up to the ball and take a few deep breaths into your centre.

Swing as slowly as possible, staying relaxed throughout the motion and breathing normally.

Take at least 30 seconds to complete your swing, without resisting the slowness or anticipating the finish.

Time yourself using the stopwatch function on your mobile; 30 seconds is much longer than you think.

Fully engage with the balance and rhythm of your swing, paying particular attention to the lower body and maintaining some awareness in your physical centre.

Try to sense how your upper body (waist, shoulders and arms) *responds* to the signals or instructions from your lower body (feet and legs) and follow its impetus rather than leading the movement.

When you relax your torso and let the weight of the legs support you, you will feel the correct kinetic sequence (feet, waist, hands), which is quite different to deliberately moving through various swing positions initiated by the arms as you follow a list of instructions in your mind. You will also feel the rotation of the t'an tien as it encourages the torso to turn.

When you can comfortably take 30 seconds to perform your swing, take 45 then 60 seconds, and when you can do this, try it with your eyes closed. This will test your proprioception, the brain's map of how it sees your body moving in space.

SLOW-MOTION TENNIS DRILLS

Practise open and closed stances, backhand and forehand and service drills, paying attention to your preparation, the moment of impact and your follow-through – all while working on the following natural movement principles:

Keep your joints stacked, especially the hips over your knees and your knees in line with your ankles.

Feel the separation from your rear foot to full extension of your lead hand holding the racket to create more elastic energy and quicker recoil.

Distinguish between hips and waist to create more torque; this is one of the key components of developing what Martina Navratilova describes as 'escalation' in the serve, which is powered from the bigger muscles and from the lower body upwards.

Keep your shoulder down on the forehand strike and generate power from your legs and centre of gravity.

Be aware of the position of the butt end of the racket; it is usually opposite the t'an tien at the moment of impact.

Start each movement transferring the weight, moving through the waist and letting your upper body and the racket head follow, thus creating a lag effect and a more whip-like motion. Tai Chi wisdom tells us that the upper and lower body don't move together but sequentially.

To emit explosive power (*Fa Jing*), there needs to be a distinction between the quality of energy at preparation and impact: these should be soft, or Yin, and hard, or Yang, respectively. Say quietly to yourself, 'Loosen, empty – strike' to help attain a state of relaxed readiness at preparation before you accelerate through the ball.

Stay focused on your t'an tien throughout the drill to encourage deep breathing, relaxed concentration (ie flow) and lower-body stability.

Do six to ten repetitions of each drill, focusing on one of the above points. Don't try to practise everything at once. The slower you can practise these drills, the better. When you feel you've mastered the drills, try adhering to the principles when hitting balls with a partner.

As you may know, Ben Hogan's golf swing has been cited as one of the greatest of all time, and it's true that he regularly practised in slow motion. Many years later, Tiger Woods would comment that (along with Moe Norman) Hogan owned his swing probably more than any other golfer, and this is precisely because of the awareness fostered by moving through his swing slowly and purposefully.

Principle Five: Listening

Over many years of Kung Fu and Tai Chi train-ing, particularly when working with groups and doing two-person drills like pushing hands or sticky hands (*Chi Sao*), listening has been a key concept for developing greater awareness.

This includes listening to one's own body, noticing tightness or tension in particular (which demonstrates nerves and gives the opponent the advantage) and maintaining composure, thus guarding against sig-nalling an attack. These unique exercises entail close proximity to your partner, with just your wrists or forearms touching, in a form of controlled spar-ring wherein you respond to the other person's intention, either absorbing or redirecting their force or pulling them off balance if they press too hard. They in turn respond to your intention and, over many years' experience, the movements made and sensed become smaller and more refined. In Wing Chun, particularly, both practitioners can be blindfolded to further heighten sensitivity. The training is fascinating because this level of awareness has a different kind of wisdom from the mind, and it can be useful for helping athletes perform under pressure, as it helps put you in touch with how your body feels. This might sound simple enough, but when you consider that nerves, adrenaline and mental interference block the connection to the body (which of course is why athletes can't move well in these situations), learning to listen for signs and symptoms of stress is a key step in overcoming them.

Avoiding stress

In the chapter Overcoming Performance Anxiety, I listed some of the responses I received from my clients and readers when I asked them what pressure feels like. You'll recall that most people talked about clear biofeedback signs like feeling nervous, the body tightening, the stomach tying in knots, getting angry and so forth, and that these symptoms lead to all kinds of self-interference from worrying about what others think to lacking the confidence to commit to shots and movement routines.

You'll know by now that the order in which pressure adversely affects performance is clear once you look at sport through this new vantage point of the mind–body connection. Leaving the mental game and psychology to one side, you clearly see the following chain reaction:

1. Performance deterioration begins with shallow breathing or even holding the breath, as I've seen some golfers do when teeing off in a tournament.

2. This triggers the stress response (nerves, anxiety and adrenaline), which causes the mind to seek coherence and recall negative thought associations, including mental images of things going wrong.

3. This leads to a lack of confidence, rushing preparation and expecting a bad result.

4. All of the above adversely affects your movement.

Listening to your body helps catch the first signs of stress and can stop the unravelling of the mind–body connection. To this end, your Performance Practice can help you develop more self-awareness and give you the tools to re-establish your composure before you begin your routine or take your shot.

TRY THIS: Biofeedback

Listen to what your body's trying to tell you. Any signs of unease can be brought under your control by finding your natural breathing rhythm, connecting to your centre and feeling your feet beneath you. Remember that this isn't a given but requires an intentional redirection of your attention away from the stress signals the biofeedback from your body is giving you, and towards a more collected state of inner quietude and relaxed readiness.

When you commit to your daily practice of seated and standing meditation and include the slow-motion drills, you'll hone an inner condition of quiet awareness that is more conducive to getting in flow than any amount of positive thinking.

Soon it will only take a few moments for you to notice the signs of stress and overcome them with your training before proceeding with your shot or routine.

Principle Six:
Self-observation

S elf-observation is a method I use with my clients. It is one of the most important steps to overcoming any challenges associated with performing under pressure, because once you begin to observe how you think, feel and act, you start the process of reversing negative and restricting behaviours that can undermine your true ability.

It's important to understand that this is not a psychological intervention and you're not looking to reframe negative thoughts or use positive self-talk; it's simply the act of observing what is going on in your body, your mind and your breathing.

Seeing the effects of nerves and anxiety and all the mental chatter without trying to stop them, alter them or push them away causes a subtle change in and of itself. Looking through the lens of the observer mind or the witness (known as the Purusha in Vedic philosophy) means you're already slightly detached from the negative effects of stress, a little freer, and if you can stay with this process while keeping some connection with your body and breathing, your biochemistry will gently move into the relaxation response.

As you self-observe, you stop identifying with the experience, ie the signs and symptoms that pressure arouses, and simply watch – alert, open and active in a wider, more objective state.

When you identify wholly with the feelings of anxiety and thoughts of the negative consequences of missing your shot, there is no space for flow to appear. As you watch your breath in meditation and find a feeling of calm settles over you, so you can watch all the nervous tension and negative mental chatter that arises before going through your movement routine. Simply by the real-time application of your various Performance Practices, such as holding to the centre or using your breathing to control your biochemistry, you will invite the same experience in the midst of competition.

In its most basic sense, self-observation – the 'big eye' – is the ability to impartially witness your moods, emotions and thoughts, as if you were observing yourself from behind a camera. At first, playing the twin roles of the observer and the observed is challenging, but over time you can learn to retain some attention within while going through your pre-shot routine. Here are some exercises to get you started.

Exercise One: Walking to the first tee

Objectives: To become more aware of your mood, thoughts and physical responses to anxiety when walking to the first tee and to begin to understand how you react to this stressful situation.

Instructions: Prior to the start of your game, practise slow, deep breathing to gain presence and awareness of your mind, body and emotions. Simply observe and notice what is going on without criticising or commenting to yourself. Immediately following your first tee shot, ask yourself the following questions:

- What was I feeling as I walked to the tee?

- What were my exact thoughts? What was my inner dialogue?

- How did I show up to this particular game? What was my mood?

- Did I notice my breathing or was I too busy thinking?

The idea is to become an observer of your traits in a moment of intense pressure so you can see how they impact your movement skills. Observe yourself without judgement, and then take a few moments to reflect and learn which of the Performance Practice methods can be most useful in these situations.

Exercise Two: Sports practice session

Objectives: To become more aware of what you are and are not accomplishing during your practice session and of how you talk to yourself about the outcomes and consequences of this.

Instructions: Stop twice during your practice session (midway and at the end) and ask yourself the following questions.

- What specific, observable outcome did I produce in my practice shot or routine?

- What excuses, stories or justifications do I have for not producing the desired outcomes?

- What got in the way of these outcomes (thoughts, feelings, inability to relax etc)?

- How can I incorporate my chosen Performance Practice methods to help me?

Exercise Three: Enhancing your performance

Objective: To create your own self-observation exercises with the intent of bettering your performance under pressure.

Instructions: Follow these simple steps.

1. Identify a challenge or block you have in your game. What makes you most anxious?

2. Aim to divide your attention in two: the observer and the observed. What do you see?

3. Look for default symptoms, patterns and trends; these will be your biofeedback signals.

4. Brainstorm in your journal for 10 minutes on how you think, feel and act under pressure.

5. Decide which Performance Practice methods are most useful for you and recommit.

Do this exercise during and immediately after your next competition or tournament; even if you don't win, you will learn something valuable for next time and will ascend in stature as an athlete.

Principle Seven:
Making Time

When my book *Breathe Golf: The missing link to a winning performance* was published in April 2019, the latest research suggested that due to the incessant chatter of the mind and the scattered rather than focused attention that seems predominant in human beings at this juncture in our development, the 'moment of now' could be accessed for a brief period of about 12 seconds.

This short time window has now decreased to around 8 seconds. You only have to look around you to see why this is so. The majority of people pay no attention to where they are or what they're doing, whether it's walking down the street or through a forest, pushing a child in a buggy, riding horseback, cycling, paying at the supermarket checkout, working out at the gym or even crossing a busy road; everyone, it seems, is always scrolling on their phone.

I recently invested in a professional turntable and speakers because I adore vinyl and wanted something top-quality to play my extensive record collection on. It's so wonderful to slow down and listen to the whole A side and then the B side of an album while appreciating the cover artwork, photos and lyrics; it's like an event, a space and time to simply be and enjoy.

Shortly afterwards, I was chatting with my neighbour about her experience with her brand-new smart speaker, which can instantly play any song she tells it to. When I asked if she listened to any of the songs the whole way through, she said no, never.

Intentional effort

In your Performance Practice, you're training yourself to be more in the moment than the general population and this is crucial for you as someone who loves sport and wants to excel in competitive situations. To this end, an *intentional effort* is required, one that goes against the seemingly natural inclination to let the mind wander and do its own thing.

Your body can only be free enough to move the way you want it to – through any complex sequence whether it's the golf swing, the jump shot or the triple

Salchow in figure skating – when your mind lets go of the past and future. Sometimes this happens by accident when a sublime shot seems to come from nowhere or when you're otherwise in flow quite spontaneously.

Being in your breathing, bringing the awareness to the t'an tien and feeling the sensation of your body are the *only* ways to get intentionally and deliberately close to this experience; otherwise, you're in the realm of thinking about thinking (mental game and psychology) and thinking about moving (worrying about getting your technique right).

The moments before you throw, begin your routine or start your edge jump are the most crucial moments of all if you want to perform well under pressure. In these few short seconds, there is an opportunity to bring all the learning from your Performance Practice together and allow yourself to enter the highly coveted state of relaxed concentration.

TRY THIS: Holding the attention within

In the moments before you take your shot, begin your routine, or as you're waiting for the starting gun, make the effort to keep your mind within your body and breathing for those few vital seconds.

If possible, feel how your body is primed into a relaxed but ready state by bringing your attention within and keeping it there rather than letting your thoughts and emotions run wild.

When it's time to move, allow your body to respond
to a clear and simple intention, letting go of any
attachment to the results. Stay with your breathing and
your centre and maintain a relaxed awareness for the
duration of the shot, routine or race.

Remember that you can't force this any more than you can force the perfect tee shot or an effortless backhand pass, but you can *invite* it if you work with this brief but essential time window. When your movement emerges from a more collected state, the quality naturally improves.

When it's time to perform, you must make room for flow to appear, put your thinking mind to one side and get out of your own way. To help yourself, you can listen, self-observe, assess the biofeedback from your body and apply your chosen methods to bring mind, body and breathing together in those few moments before any complex movement begins. These are the moments all your effort, hard work and getting up early every morning to meditate have been leading up to.

Principle Eight:
Just Enough

This is another key concept I've learned over many years of martial arts training; it's a simple law of motion, particularly in a stressful situation, that I see being broken again and again by athletes of all levels in competition whether grassroots or elite.

Watching Andy Murray versus Novak Djokovic in the 2015 Australian Open men's final, I noticed there was a moment when a jaded-looking Djokovic seemed out of the picture from a slip after a full stretch to return Andy's serve, and all the Scot had to do was get the ball back in the ad court (the left side) and he would win the point. Like many who've been in a similar situation, he overcooked it, tried too hard and the ball slammed into the net, giving Djokovic the advantage and, ultimately, his fifth championship title.

There are many examples like this from any sport you care to mention, but this stayed with me as evidence that just enough energy, just enough force, just enough commitment and just enough movement are all that's needed when you're under pressure.

Any more than just enough brings the opposite result to the one you intended. What you don't want to do in these situations is bring too much muscle to your movement or think too much about what you need to achieve; simply trust your body to respond to the situation in the moment.

Economy of movement

In Kung Fu when you block an opponent's punch or move your head out of the way of an attacker's blow, your head needs to be only just far enough away that they can't reach you. To do this, you need to be fully aware of both your own body in space and your opponent's intention.

Many useful things result from this, such as economy of motion, conserving energy, remaining in balance and a quick recovery. Beginners often overdo it, not only telegraphing their punches but also overreacting and embellishing what should be a quick, simple and efficient movement when blocking or evading an attack.

When you're in flow, everything's just right – you have all the time you need to execute the shot, move or routine, you don't try too hard, you don't think too much, and there's a quiet confidence in your abilities. It doesn't matter if you're a junior, a weekend warrior, a committed club player or a world-class superstar, flow is available to any athlete at any time provided they meet certain conditions: unity of mind, body and motion.

TRY THIS: A light touch

Hold to the principle of 'just enough' in your next sports practice session. Feel how this simple shift in attention and controlled effort creates greater freedom of motion and allows you to release your complex movement skills in the most natural way.

Using your practice of self-observation, check in with yourself from time to time throughout your next competition to make sure you're not gripping the baseball bat, snooker cue, golf club or tennis-racket too tight.

Holding on lightly with just the right amount of tension and no more sends a strong signal to your brain and nervous system that you're on top of the situation and as a result you'll activate the relaxation response and a wider, calmer mental state.

Your Performance Practice can help you emulate the relaxed but ready quality of *just enough* in your day-to-day training so it can manifest when you're under pressure to give yourself absolutely every possible chance for flow to appear.

Principle Nine:
Wonder And Awe

All the athletes I've worked with who've experienced the flow state or zone, together with hundreds, even thousands of others around the world whose comments have been documented over the past few decades, report that this extraordinary state renders the complex movements involved in sport completely effortless.

I've even coached junior tennis players of around eleven years of age who knew all about flow and told me during our first meeting that while in this experience, they had seen the tennis ball rotating as if in slow motion, coming over the net towards them, and that they felt they had all the time in the world to get into position and hit an unreturnable shot.

It's easy to see when an athlete is in flow even when watching sport on television; there is an unmistakable, captivating quality to their movement, and this is one of the reasons why sport is loved so much by athletes and spectators alike. It gives us a glimpse of what's possible for human beings once we put the limiting mind and ego to one side and allow a higher intelligence to emerge.

Although mainstream commentators won't talk about inner stillness when discussing an athlete's top form and sublime movement skills (they will most likely put it down to mental toughness and good technique), as you develop your Performance Practice, you'll begin to appreciate how flow manifests in your daily meditation, life and sport, and you'll spot this state more and more in other athletes.

In the majority of sports, there's no real threat or consequence to failure; missing a goal kick, a snooker pot or a golfing putt might bruise the ego and affect the scores on the board, but usually it's not a matter of life or death. Other sports, however, such as motor racing, base jumping, slacklining, skiing and free climbing, are on a knife-edge between success and complete disaster, and in these situations, flow is not only more apparent but also more necessary.

The role of humility

I'm a big fan of winter sports and coach a lot of skiers, and I love watching the big slalom races, especially when there's that fine margin of hundredths of a second between the contenders who have to stay just the right side of gravity, almost like controlled falling, feeling the forces of nature as they interact with their body and the skis.

I remember vividly one competition with Lindsey Vonn, winner of four World Cup overall championships. Watching her was like seeing water pouring down the side of a mountain; the combination of intense focus plus relaxation rendered her movement unlike that of any of her rivals.

Many athletes who are sadly no longer with us have only been able to surpass what we'd consider to be the bounds of human capabilities by being in flow.

As recounted in Christopher Hilton's book *Inside the Mind of the Grand Prix Driver*, the inimitable Formula One driver, Ayrton Senna, experienced flow, or being in the zone, long before these terms became common parlance in sport. Senna said of his experience behind the wheel that the faster he drove, the slower everything seemed to get.

The late Dean Potter, who enjoyed soloing on a slackline at 7,500 feet from Taft Point in Yosemite following his daily meditation and Yoga practice, could never even have attempted such incredible and almost superhuman feats without being in the moment.

Keeping a sense of wonder and maintaining a little humility in the face of the experiences of the flow state and the zone, which are gifted to human beings and are not obliged to appear on demand of the ego and will, is crucial.

A client recently asked if I could offer him some intensive coaching to help him manage his many and varied business roles as well as improve his golf. He stated that he wanted to 'master getting into the state of flow', which, as I gently pointed out, is not only impossible but also anathema to what he was seeking.

TRY THIS: Letting go of the future

If you start to feel anxious about an upcoming event or tournament, immediately bring your awareness to the moment you're in, without worrying about how you're going to perform in a few weeks' time. Remember that the only way to prepare yourself for being present on the golf course or on the high beam in gymnastics is to practise being in the moment you're in, again and again and again.

Any time you can bring your attention to your breathing, you can make the effort to stay with it and thus quieten your thoughts. Any time you can remember your body, you have the opportunity to let your mind rest in the hara or feel the ground beneath your feet. Whenever you remember to observe yourself, you can gain a little distance from your emotions and enjoy a widening of your mind.

All this is conducive to ascending the ranks in the sport you love in real-time competitive situations.

Flow is a mysterious state which many athletes, dancers, musicians and performers have described as otherworldly, extraordinary, even spiritual, as it takes us into another realm. Being *present*, in the now, is not a given: you must work towards it, and then allow it to manifest itself, transcending thought and time, without getting impatient if it doesn't show up.

It's a tough pill to swallow but once you've been in flow you can't recreate it from the ordinary conditions of the thinking mind; you can only stay with the process of practising and aspiring to bring your mind, body and breathing together as one.

Remember that the role of an athlete embracing this new paradigm of the mind–body connection is simply to prepare the ground for the unique state of flow, or the zone, to appear. Once the mind is quiet and the body exhibits a relaxed readiness, you'll be at the threshold of these otherworldly experiences, which will emerge as effortless movement so long as you refrain from grasping, forcing or trying too hard.

Principle Ten: Downtime And Recuperation

The changes that occur when you commit to a daily practice of breathing meditation, standing or stance training and intentional self-awareness are palpable, and these changes will affect you on so many levels that from time to time you might wish to stop for a few days to let all the new experiences settle. These are times when writing up your notes in a journal or training book is important, as you get to reflect and process for a while before continuing with the journey.

Even Buddhist monks take a break now and then, as they refrain from practising meditation on calendar days which contain the number eight. They simply go about their daily duties, like bathing, cleaning and cooking, while paying attention to their breathing as they carry out these various tasks.

As someone who loves sport, you'll know that when your body feels tired you can probably keep going. Athletes involved in extreme sports like the Triple Ironman, which entails a 7.2-mile open-water swim and a 336-mile bike ride followed by three marathons totalling 78.6 miles back to back, get used to making this extraordinary physical effort. Even doing those extra laps in the pool or a few more reps in the gym shows how the body can go beyond self-imposed and often mental limitations.

Interestingly, the zone, or flow state, often manifests itself quite spontaneously when you commit totally to your sport without restricting thoughts hampering your movement, as this feedback from reader and hurler, Dave Lewis will testify:

> *'Every time the ball came to me, I was able to pick it up and get it to my hand, and strike it clearly into the net. I knew my job and accomplished it over and over again. I was able not to worry about making mistakes or not making it to the final, but just put my head down and get into the zone, and when I did make mistakes, I let them go instead of dwelling on them. The meditation helped me not only to win a world championship but to enjoy the sport of hurling even more.'*

Reward yourself with joy

Conversely, when your mind is tired it's usually advisable to rest; these are times you can take a break from formal practice and instead go for a long walk in nature, tend to your garden, play your Xbox or guitar, do some colouring or cooking or whatever you do for relaxation while engaging in a leisurely way with your breathing and a relaxed awareness of your body.

When you're deeply immersed in a joyful activity, flow can arise quite naturally, and if you can stay with the experience for those few moments as you plant the rose bush, strum the chords of your favourite song or reach the next level in your video game, it will greatly help your daily practice when you feel ready to resume.

It's also good to mix up your training so that you sit or stand at a different time of the day or in a different room or on the floor instead of a chair. You can split a 30-minute practice into one 15-minute session of sitting followed by 15 minutes of standing, or if you really want to push yourself, you can practise when you're feeling tired, hungry, irritable or emotional so that you need to make an extra effort to follow your breathing or witness your thoughts.

As you can gather, this work is completely different from a 2-minute mindfulness exercise and requires consistent effort, which can often be a tremendous inner struggle, so it's OK to take a few days off now and then.

What I wouldn't advise and could be detrimental to your overall development is to force your Performance Practice either when there isn't enough time and you're struggling to manage your schedule or when you're feeling unwell and need to rest.

You need to know the difference between copping out, ie avoiding doing what you know you should be doing, and needing some downtime. You can then continue with your training, going deeper into the extraordinary phenomena of the meditative state and understanding more and more what's required of you for this to exhibit itself at times when you need to excel under pressure.

PART THREE
TWELVE-WEEK MIND–BODY PERFORMANCE CHALLENGE

'A warrior must take care only that his will remains unbroken, that the principles of his art are applied in his life, and that he recognises his heart in his daily activities.'
— **Chozan Shissai**, *A Discourse on the Art of Swordsmanship*, in R Kammer, *Zen and Confucius in the Art of Swordsmanship*

Introduction To
The Challenge

The twin passions of my life over the past three decades have been Tai Chi (the world's most popular martial art) and fitness training. I've done everything from running, cycling, swimming, circuit training and rowing and I continue to practise martial arts daily and swim or do body weight exercises at home several times per week. I also practise seated meditation each morning for 30 minutes and extend this practice into long walks through the park at the weekend.

I've been captivated since I was a teenager by the grace and power found in sporting movements. After several decades of training and researching and developing my ideas, this fascination has only increased along with the understanding of how to help those who love sport dispel all forms of self-interference and release their complex movement skills when it matters. I also lead a team of coaches who are helping athletes across the world enter this new era of the mind–body connection.

For many years this was a labour of love, and perhaps because most coaches in golf and sport are male and I had some *alternative* ideas, it was a real struggle to be heard for the first ten years or more.

This was especially so in the golf industry, which has been dominated by a left-brain approach to improving performance, consisting mainly of thinking about technique and, of course, the so-called mental game. Having officially launched my business in 2004, I'm pleased to say there are now thousands of golfers in over twenty countries around the world training the Chi Performance way.

Many athletes, even those at the Olympic and professional level, tighten up in competition, with the result that the moves and routines and ball striking they can usually perform perfectly in practice or when there's nothing at stake simply fall apart. We've seen this in golf umpteen times, we've seen it in tennis, in athletics, in football, in snooker and in every other sport you care to mention. Why is this so?

Well, for one thing we know that the mainstream approach to sports performance still treats and trains the mind and body separately. Athletes have a mental game coach helping them to think about how they're thinking as well as a technical coach to teach them how to think about the mechanics of the ball toss or golf swing and so on. Neither of these interventions helps in any consistent way to raise performance levels or dispel the negative effects of pressure. It is a separatist approach which does nothing to quieten the mind or deepen the breathing, both of which serve to relax the body and allow movement to emerge in a way that's free, natural and spontaneous.

How the challenge was born

The idea for this Twelve-week Mind–Body Performance Challenge came about in the autumn of 2019 long before there was any indication that our world was about to change.

One of my American students, Tom (a golfer based in Washington), whom I'd worked with online for several months, came to meet me in the UK during one of his business trips to Europe. He was interested in a longer-term approach, not only to raising his performance on the golf course but also to the best way of losing weight, shaping up and treating a troubling knee injury. His overall focus was to develop a morning routine which would 'upgrade my daily life pattern'.

I put together a simple plan for Tom, based on my own approach to fitness and daily training, which goes back over more than three decades and incorporates both Eastern and Western disciplines and exercises which I have done continually during that time.

After getting approval from his physician (a leading expert who has given performance advice to the Washington Commanders and thought the Twelve-week Challenge was excellent), Tom got some great results, which included him losing a stone in weight inside the first month and getting relief from his painful knee.

I then decided to roll out the programme to other people in sport who wanted to use the enforced lockdowns to raise their overall fitness, as daily life as we had known it came to a standstill in the spring of 2020.

This Twelve-week Mind–Body Performance Challenge seemed more imperative than ever, as it presented a way for many people to 'lean in' to this epic event, to step up and use the silence, the stillness, and in many cases the solitude imposed by external events to do as my Washington client said and upgrade our daily life patterns.

Many clients used this Twelve-week Challenge to hone their Performance Practice, staying strong, centred and prepared for their sporting comeback when football pitches, gyms, tennis courts and stadiums reopened to the public.

What's interesting about many of the Eastern practices you're going to adopt as part of a new daily routine is that for a long time I promoted their benefits only in terms of strengthening the mind–body connection for enhanced sports performance; however, they have numerous health and wellbeing benefits too, including helping to reduce stress, raising energy levels, preventing injury and burnout, boosting the immune system and overcoming anxiety issues.

These additional benefits, plus of course the self-determination it takes to complete such a challenge, are even more important following Covid-19, as the world is becoming increasingly destabilised through wars, famine, the rising costs of food and essentials, and an ever-escalating refugee crisis.

This Twelve-week Mind–Body Performance Challenge is also a response to watching gym-goers and people who enjoy fitness and physique development zone out into the TV screens when on the treadmill or spin bike, and weightlifters losing valuable focus by scrolling through their phones between sets. It seems nobody under the age of about thirty can survive for more than a few minutes without checking their social media.

Here's the first thing to understand about the mind–body connection and begin to hold as the benchmark against which you measure the quality of every activity. When you train your muscle with weights – let's say you're doing dumbbell curls to pump up your biceps – you can get 60% more muscle gains over time using a lighter weight, but with your attention focused on your biceps rather than the latest celebrity chat show or Instagram pictures of what your mates are having for lunch.

This goes part way to explaining what the mind–body connection is. It's not an idea or a fleeting thought about balance or breathing when lifting weights, running or playing tennis; it's about bringing some attention and awareness to the physical sensation of the body, feeling your torso supported by your legs, or your feet on the floor, or your chest emptying and your breath deep in the lower abdomen and *staying there* for the few moments it takes to quieten down inside.

The aim of the challenge

The aim of this challenge is to help you streamline every aspect of your training so you can prepare yourself in a unified and holistic way for performing at your best in high-pressure situations in competitive sport. You're going to transform your diet, nutrition and supplementation plan, as well as your cardio-vascular, strength, conditioning and sports-specific workouts, based on an understanding of the biochemistry of performance and the biomechanics of natural movement.

These principles include learning how to breathe more efficiently, quietening your mind, developing greater balance and leg strength, activating your body's centre of gravity for more power and precision, and accessing the zone, or flow state, so that your movement can emerge unimpeded by worry, anxiety and all forms of mental interference.

This Twelve-week Mind–Body Performance Challenge is also an antidote to the popular fad of mindfulness, which for most people simply means listening to an app with some guided imagery on their smartphone. As you know, I give little credence to these gimmicks, as they require minimal effort on the part of the user and remain only a superficial help and one aligned to a psychological approach.

What's on offer here is the chance to go deeper by making an intentional effort to quieten your mind with formal meditation, for when the mind is quiet the body can move naturally and efficiently with grace and power.

Becoming the best version of yourself isn't an option any more, it's a necessity. Your family, friends, colleagues, teammates and the rest of humanity needs you to undergo this journey of continuous self-improvement, if not radical transformation. This is necessary not for the outer personality with its ego strivings but for the inside, through stillness and a calm equanimity so you don't get tossed around by external events and instead steer your own course whenever possible.

Perhaps most importantly, you will take back your precious attention – which global corporations and social media platforms now vie for as some sort of commodity – by working moment to moment to bring your focus firmly back within yourself.

Please be patient and honour the journey you're about to take. I've been working with these principles and practices my whole life and have been coaching others for over two decades, so go slowly and rest assured you are in safe hands.

Before you begin

Before you start the challenge it's important that you identify your specific goals in each of the following Eight Keys to Mind–Body Training:

1. Diet, nutrition, hydration and supplementation

2. Cardiovascular fitness and conditioning

3. Suppleness and fascia stretching

4. Lower-body strength and stability

5. Upper-body softness and flexibility

6. Activation of the t'an tien

7. Seated and standing meditation

8. Raising your Chi, or energy levels

You might also want to do some additional preparation with keys One and Seven, diet and meditation, as that's where we're going to begin.

Also think about taking a full-length photo of yourself *before* the challenge starts so you can compare it with your physique, fitness and general demeanour when you finish.

In addition to looking and feeling better and having more energy, by ramping up their fitness training, many athletes have told me that their spouses, children or teammates notice a difference in them as they make meditation part of their daily routine and become kinder, less angry and more patient with others.

Your daily practice will include seated or standing meditation, slow and intentional awareness when eating, mind–muscle connection while weight training, and breath-centred cardio workouts.

Your weekly practice will include energy training (the literal translation of Chi Kung) and t'an tien exercises, fascia stretching, slow-motion drills, integrating your Performance Practice with your sports practice, writing up your journal and making a plan for the week ahead.

As we continue week on week, I'll explain everything, including all the unfamiliar terms, what you'll be doing, why you'll be doing it, what feedback to look out for and, of course, the results you can expect. You can rest one day each week, enjoy the downtime and eat what you like. You will find action plans at the end of most weeks to help you.

Why are you going to begin this challenge with your diet and meditation? Well, what you eat and how much you eat accounts for an astonishing 70% of your body mass index, so it's important to get this right before jumping into an exercise routine.

As this challenge is specifically about developing the all-important mind–body connection, you are also going to become more *mindful* of how you eat. As I've already said that my work is opposed to the modern trend of mindfulness, let me quantify that.

Whenever the word 'mindful' is used in this book and specifically in the Twelve-week Challenge, it is to denote a state of intentionally redirecting your attention towards your breathing and physical body, particularly the hara. Even more importantly, it denotes the attempt to retain some attention there for a short amount of time, while performing daily activities, until an inner quietude is established.

With regards to eating your meals, this will include moments of sustained effort to follow the breath or relax into the body, awakening the twin qualities of steadfastness (*Sthira*) and ease (*Sukha*) spoken of in

Vedic literature. Doing so reduces the internal chatter, calms excessive emotions and keeps your mood elevated, as it promotes a deep inner peace and feeling of joy. Your food will taste much better too.

In your daily meditations, you will adopt one of the oldest and simplest approaches already outlined in Part Two, which is to follow the breathing while holding some awareness in the lower abdomen. You will also be doing a form of standing meditation practice, which brings the synergy of the quiet Zen mind together with a sense of relaxed physical power and is ideal for athletes seeking the internal conditions which always exist prior to the execution of effortless movement.

Developing the state of relaxed readiness, or *sung*, which is the pre-fight readiness of martial artists, can be helpful when setting up over the ball, waiting with your shotgun for the trap to be released, or standing poolside before diving into the water. It can be trained no matter what you're doing, and since many people use mealtimes for screen time, this will be a good, although difficult, first attempt.

Now let's begin your Twelve-week Mind–Body Performance Challenge.

Week One

In the first week, prepare a new training journal dedicated to your Twelve-week Challenge where you can log your progress and record any observations so that you can review, make adjustments and steer your course to ensure you get the best results.

Start by writing out your intended outcomes for the challenge and, if you wish, you can share these with a partner, friend or teammate – someone you love and trust and who wants the best for you – thus gaining their valuable support and encouragement.

You might need to review your current diet and make any necessary changes to your weekly shopping list, including what you have available in your kitchen from main meals to snacks.

Begin to notice not only what you eat but also *how you eat*; try to consume each meal slowly and with intentional self-awareness to bring yourself more into the present moment and to get the most energy and enjoyment from your food.

In the past, you may have eaten quickly while watching TV or continuing to work at your desk. Now is the chance to slow down and appreciate that, as one client said, a meal is a series of small, tasty mouthfuls to savour as opposed to a plate of food to get through as quickly as possible.

This is also a great way to start losing a few pounds if you need to, as rather than eating a huge dessert which you pay little attention to, eating a smaller dessert while focusing on the pleasurable taste and the act of bringing the spoon to your mouth and back to the bowl means you don't need to eat so much to get the same feeling of satisfaction and fullness.

In Week One you will also want to prepare yourself for a daily seated meditation by rereading the guide in Part Two of this book. Once you've reviewed the practice (which, in his book *Zen Mind, Beginner's Mind*, Zen master Shunryu Suzuki calls 'the fundamental practice of every human being'), you might wish to write out why you are committed to daily meditation and decide when you are going to start. You don't need to have outlandish ideas about the results you want to attain, just a simple goal of sitting for 20 minutes in the morning before going to work will be challenging enough.

When you begin, keep things simple, don't try too hard and avoid looking for results; for example, don't sit in the morning and then get annoyed if you play a poor round of golf in the afternoon. Anything transformative takes time. For now, you are simply building a daily routine of at least 15–20 minutes, sitting quietly breathing in and breathing out naturally without changing anything or seeking to control your breath in any way. Simply observe how it comes and goes without anything being needed from you.

Your minimum challenge is four meditation sessions per week, although ideally you should be practising every day, so use this first week to make the necessary adjustments to help you schedule the practice into your routine. There's no doubt it will be difficult – you may be hungry, or tired in the morning, or you may have to find some quiet time in the evening when others in your household are enjoying a movie – but this extra effort will be worth it as you adjust your routine to support your ascent as an athlete and a human being.

If you are already doing a daily meditation practice, try to sit for longer (up to 30 minutes) and begin the process of staying mindful of your breathing *after* your meditation session has ended. For instance, witness your breathing when getting up from your cushion and walking through the house, making a drink, writing up your journal or preparing breakfast.

When you start doing standing meditation (which in the challenge begins in Week Four), you can alternate this with your seated practice. Many clients sit for three mornings in a row followed by a session of standing. Elite golf clients like to stand before tournament days and do seated meditation on days off or when travelling.

Week One action plan

Know your intended outcome

Sit quietly for a few minutes or use the time directly after meditation to get a clear picture of yourself as you would like to be when you have completed the Twelve-week Challenge. Write a full-page description of this picture, including specific details of the athlete you have decided to become, how your thinking and performance have changed, plus your achievements, triumphs and any personal issues or obstacles you've overcome.

Use affirmations and visualisation

An affirmation is a statement that describes a goal in its already-completed state. One way to guarantee you achieve your potential is to bombard your subconscious mind with thoughts and images of the athlete you want to be, imagining your physique, technical prowess, level of performance, and ability to overcome nerves in pressure situations – exactly the way you would like.

From the description you created above, write out a brief affirmation, simply stating how pleased you are with your major achievements, using the following guidelines to help:

1. Start with the words 'I am'. The subconscious mind takes any sentence that starts with these words and interprets it as a command, an instruction to make it a reality.

2. Use the present tense. Describe what you want as though you already have it, as if it is already accomplished. You could begin with 'I am so happy and grateful now that…'.

3. Affirm what you want and state your affirmations in the positive. Your energy follows your intention, so focus on the end result not the obstacles.

4. Keep it brief and be specific. It needs to be short enough to be punchy and memorable, rather like a riff from a song, and the more specific and detailed your affirmation, the better the result.

5. Include an action word. Verbs ending in '-ing' add power to your affirmative statement by evoking an image of you already being the athlete you aspire to: 'I'm living, I'm enjoying, I'm winning.'

6. Include at least one dynamic emotion or feeling word. Include a word to describe how you'd be feeling if you had already attained your desired goal.

7. Finish with the phrase 'or something better'. There might be a higher level of attainment possible, which you can't see from your present level of experience, so include the phrase 'or something better' when it feels appropriate.

8. Visualise the process as well as the outcome. As we saw with Jack Nicklaus's visualisation process in Part One, it's important to include your daily Performance Practice in your affirmations so that your goals are supported by the thing that will make them a reality; for example, 'I am enjoying my meditation and love the feeling of being in the game when my mind is quiet.'

More ways to affirm and visualise

- Review your affirmations every day. The best times are first thing in the morning after sitting in meditation, in the middle of the day to refocus, and around bedtime.

- If appropriate, read each affirmation out loud and try to stay close to your breathing and the hara centre as you do so to fully embody what you want to achieve.

- Close your eyes and visualise yourself as the affirmation describes. See it as if you were looking out at the scene; in other words, don't see yourself standing out there in the scene, see the scene as if you were actually living it.

- Hear any sounds you might hear when you successfully achieve what your affirmation describes. Include important people in your life congratulating you and telling you how pleased they are with your success.

- Feel the feelings that you will experience when you achieve that success. These feelings should be aligned with a quiet inner confidence and gratitude that is supported by your practice. This step is particularly useful if you have aphantasia and find it difficult, if not impossible, to visualise.

Daily reminders

- Write your affirmations on a postcard and carry them with you in your kitbag.

- Hang pictures of athletes and other heroes and sheroes that inspire you, especially those like Steph Curry, Novak Djokovic or three-time Olympic volleyball champion Kerri Walsh Jennings, who each have a regular meditation practice.

- Record your affirmations on your phone and listen to them when training, when preparing to compete, during downtime and / or while falling asleep.

- Put your affirmations on your screen saver on your computer, smartphone etc, so you'll see them every time you switch your devices on. They can also act as a useful reminder to witness your breathing and not to zone out into the latest gossip or trend on social media.

Week Two

B egin to make some careful observations and write up anything that stopped you following through during Week One. It might be that you need to readjust the time you sit in meditation or make more effort to stop rushing your meals, or you may need to get more support from those around you or review your daily schedule and so on.

This week you should be able to firmly establish your routine by noticing the pitfalls from Week One and making the necessary adjustments. Stay with your new eating plan and look at your hydration and supplementation needs, which will be individual to you and based on your overall goals for your fitness and physique development.

There is no right way or one-size-fits-all approach when it comes to diet, nutrition, supplementation and hydration.

My preferred diets for athletes and those involved in the health and fitness lifestyle are the low glycaemic index, food combining (where you eat your protein and carbohydrates separately), the Mediterranean diet (this is my absolute favourite and is known for having the greatest benefits for keeping your heart healthy) and Nancy Clark's *Sports Nutrition Guidebook*, which has a ton of great advice and energy-fuelled recipes. All these books are in my kitchen and inform what I eat. I'm not getting paid to promote them and I'm not a dietician, it's just what I recommend to my clients.

There are other options, including the Paleo (or Palaeolithic) diet, based on what our stone-age ancestors ate; the Keto diet, where you drastically reduce your carbohydrate intake and replace them with fats; and, of course, the increasingly popular vegan diet.

What you choose depends on your goals, so having a clear idea of your intended outcome will help you put the right plan for your needs in place. I have seen several athletes fall into the trap of exhaustion and adrenal fatigue by giving their body excess work to do in terms of processing and digesting raw food or not taking in enough calories or the right kind of food, which then overstresses the system. When you're working out with weights, running, cycling or otherwise training for your sport, be sensible and try to achieve balance in your diet.

Many people following an athletic lifestyle (including me) prefer to eat six smaller meals per day, rather than the traditional breakfast, lunch and dinner. Ideally, you'll want to eat every three hours so that your daily intake looks something like this: breakfast, mid-morning snack, lunch, mid-afternoon snack, early dinner, mid-evening snack. Eat only after your morning exercise and don't eat after 8pm. Fuelling your body regularly raises your metabolism and encourages the release of fat stores. Not eating causes the body to hold on to its fat reserves, which is why many diets don't work. You can swap a mid-evening snack for a protein shake if you're trying to build muscle.

When it comes to hydration, there is little consensus among the experts, so it's best to find out what works for you; too much water flushes out your body's electrolytes and too little water impairs cognitive as well as physical performance, so just experiment and find what's right for you as an individual.

You might also like to explore the benefits of various sports supplements. The ones I have personally found to be most effective for lean muscle gains are creatine, L-glutamine, protein shakes and branched-chain amino acids, all of which will support your physique development, especially if you are working with heavy weights.

If you're doing endurance-based cardio training, you might like to use a performance-based drink such as PhD Battery +/-_3. I am not being paid to promote this brand, but I use PhD protein blends after circuit training and PhD Battery +/-_3, which I keep pool-side while swimming.

If you don't want to spend your budget on sport supplements, you can make your own performance drink to fuel your cardio workouts by mixing a little salt in a beaker of sugar-free squash, as this will help to recharge your electrolytes and is much better for you than plain water, especially if you're putting intense effort into your training.

Week Two action plan

Following your preparatory work before beginning this Twelve-week Challenge, you should have a clear idea of your goals and know where you're headed for each of the eight keys, with keys One and Seven being your priority for now. You'll be reflecting on Week One and seeing what adjustments might be needed and will have written out your affirmations and shared them with someone you trust.

You can also review the success soundtrack you recorded in Part One to see if any changes or improvements can be made. In Week Two you'll be listening to your recording twice each day and/or when training.

Now it's time to make a vision board that reflects your affirmations in pictorial form.

Making a vision board

1. Find or download pictures of your favourite athletes, famous people who inspire you, places you love, sayings, quotations and power words.

2. The pictures should represent what you want to have, do and be, and could include images of the competitions you would like to enter, the trophies you'd like to win, and the status you'd like to achieve in your sport.

3. The images should make you feel energised; they should be relevant to you personally and resonate with your unique goals. At one time my vision board had pictures of Dame Kelly Holmes and Christine Ohuruogu, two of England's most successful female track athletes, alongside images of the Marathon Monks from Japan's Mount Hiei.

4. When you're happy with your images and have as many as you feel you need, paste them onto a large piece of board and then hang your vision board on the wall where you will see it every day.

5. As you look at your vision board, repeat your affirmations out loud and see yourself achieving all your goals. Remember to make it reflect not

just your desired outcome but the means to attain it. Include a picture of meditation or Tai Chi and try to feel your feet on the ground and your breath in the lower abdomen as you speak.

Write up your training journal

Write up your challenges, triumphs and observations in your training journal every Sunday and plan for the week ahead, adjusting your course as necessary while reaffirming your overall vision and specific goals.

Week Three

This challenge isn't necessarily about adding more to your routine but about doing less, better. For you this means organising every aspect of your preparation and performance for sport in a way that supports the development of the mind–body connection.

In Week Three you will stay with your diet, nutrition, hydration and supplementation plan, which, as you know, will account for 70% of your body mass index and at this stage is more crucial for promoting fat loss and lean muscle gains than your exercise routine, although we're going to cover that next.

You are also going to continue with your daily meditation, and as you have started to incorporate this when eating, you are now going to bring more self-awareness into your conditioning workouts, starting with cardiovascular fitness and weight, resistance or circuit training. Again, you will have identified your specific goals in these areas from the brainstorming work which formed the basis of Week One.

Cardio workouts

First, let's look at three specific types of cardio workout that you can mix and match.

1. **Tempo training:** Here the goal will be to maintain a steady state of about 60–80% of your maximum heart rate for 40–60 minutes. If you don't have a heart rate monitor that's OK, I don't use one either but prefer to tune into my body and go by what 60–80% of my maximum capacity *feels* like. If 100% capacity is a full-on sprint and 40% might be walking round a golf course, then you can judge for yourself what 60–80% of your maximum heart rate capacity feels like for you.

2. **Slow burn:** Here you will be exercising for between 1.5 and 2 hours at a slow, comfortable pace without raising your heart rate beyond 40% of its maximum capacity. This approach is proven to switch the body into an aerobic state, which helps to release fat stores and use them as fuel. It's an energising and invigorating way to train,

and ideally you'll want to include this approach in your overall routine.

3. **High-intensity interval training:** Here you will do between four and seven short bursts of between 90–100% of your maximum heart rate capacity with slightly longer rest intervals at a moderate intensity; for example, you can do 60 second high-intensity bursts with 2 minute rest intervals or (one of my favourites) you can adopt the 'pyramid' approach where you will do 30, 60, 90 and 120 seconds of high-intensity bursts with short rest intervals followed by another 90, 60 and 30 second intense bursts, also with rest intervals.

Please note that you must *keep moving* during the rest intervals but at a much slower pace so you can get your breath back, let your heart rate slow down and prepare yourself for another all-out effort. You can use a stationary bike, cross trainer (sometimes called an elliptical), treadmill or rowing machine, or go outside and try alternating running and sprinting, walking and jogging or cycling up and down hills.

To help you develop your mind–body connection during your cardio workouts, try staying focused on the t'an tien. Maintaining your focus in this area will help you to breathe more deeply and slowly, the importance of which to delivering fluid movement when you're under pressure we've already discussed. We'll further explore the role of the t'an tien in Week

Five, but for now practise bringing mind and body together by focusing on this area just below the navel while working out.

You may notice that when your attention is drawn in this way to the lower abdomen, you begin to breathe more efficiently, which has the effect of raising your available oxygen levels, helping you to train for longer and recover more quickly.

It also helps to keep your mind quiet, and this will give you more energy to bring to your sport. For example, a swimming client told me she won a race by focusing on breathing deeply into her t'an tien instead of worrying about her competitor in the next lane with whom she was neck and neck. Countless others have reported similar experiences. Following your breathing helps reduce anxiety, keeps all that mental interference to a minimum and gives you additional energy which would otherwise be wasted.

Strength training

First you will need to get a set of weights and a bench or join the local gym if you're not already a member. Your equipment can be as simple or as elaborate as your budget allows. I use a set of dumbbells and an EZ curl bar plus an adjustable bench at home, but I also like to use kettlebells and a medicine ball and do body weight workouts using the TRX suspension equipment at the gym.

Your next task is to identify first whether you are going to do weight, resistance or circuit training, and second the specific exercises you're going to do, making sure they are all functional movements and, if possible, that they are related in some way to your sport.

Of course, you'll need to pay attention to the muscle or group of muscles being worked to get those extra performance gains by strengthening the mind–body connection. This is yet another reason why your regular meditation is such a useful practice.

If you want to build muscle, that is to increase the size or the density of the muscle you currently have, you're going to want to opt for weight training and use fewer repetitions but with more weight. Ideally, you will train one or two body parts per day, alternating the bigger muscles of your back, for example, with a smaller muscle like your biceps, or the larger muscles of the chest with the smaller triceps.

Basic exercises like squats, deadlifts, bench presses and pull-ups help trigger the entire musculature of the body to grow, so you could stick with these fundamentals for four to six weeks before incorporating additional drills. Some might consider it retro, as we live in an age when everyone wants a fitness app, but if you *can* go old-school (and it didn't do Arnold Schwarzenegger any harm) and simply work on the above, including compound movements like

power cleans and snatches and some additional ply-
ometrics such as box jumps, you'll be working both
slow and fast twitch muscle fibres for strength and
explosiveness.

Make sure you take enough rest days, as this is when
your muscle grows while repairing itself after the
punishing loads you've given it.

If you want to build your overall strength *without* gaining extra muscle but just toning up the muscle you
already have, then opt for resistance training with
moderate weights and a medium number of repetitions, ideally somewhere between eight and twelve.
The most efficient way to tone up is to train your upper
body one day, your lower body the next day, and to
ideally do a cardio workout on the third day before
beginning the cycle again.

Finally, if, like me, you want to get the best possible
gains in the shortest possible workout time, then opt
for circuit training where you train the entire body in
a single session using either lighter weights and more
reps or heavy weights and fewer reps. Some serious
weightlifters I know even do a one- or two-rep maximum for each muscle, whereas I aim to do twelve to
fifteen reps using lighter weights or simply my body
weight. The order I have followed for many years
is legs, biceps, chest, triceps, back, abdominals and
shoulders – all in a single workout.

Exercises

There is a lot of material available online about how to work out safely with free weights, so please check and do your own research. Ideally, you'll be doing the following exercises:

- **For your legs**, you'll want to do a combination of squats, such as front squats, goblet squats, Romanian or one-legged squats, plus lunges, leg presses, deadlifts and calf raises.

- **For your biceps**, you'll be doing dumbbell, kettlebell, cable or barbell curls with different grips (wide or narrow) and varying tempos.

- **For your chest**, you'll want to do push-ups, including incline push-ups where you raise your feet up on a bench or a chair, plus bench presses and dumbbell flys.

- **For your triceps**, you'll do dips, overhead extension, French presses and close presses either with the weights or as an adapted push-up with your hands much closer together than usual.

- **For your back**, you can do pull-ups if you have somewhere high you can grab hold of and pull yourself up (I've done all sorts of things over the years, like using my loft or bolting a bar into the door frame). You can also do bent-over barbell rows and single-arm dumbbell rows.

- **For your abdominals**, crunches are the thing, either with your feet flat on the floor or, if you want to make life a bit harder for yourself, with your lower legs raised up onto a chair and a flat plate of between 5 kilograms and 10 kilograms placed on your chest so you have extra weight to crunch. I would also recommend you do some additional core work like the plank and Superman (which of course I like to call Superwoman), where you will use your core muscles to hold yourself in position for anywhere between 30 seconds to around 2–3 minutes.

- **For your shoulders**, you will use barbell and dumbbell presses, either seated or standing, as well as upright rows with the cable machine or dumbbells and lateral flies to ensure you work all three heads of the deltoid muscle.

Please go slowly and use good form when doing your training. Try to use *explosive* power when lifting or pushing the weight, perhaps pausing for a moment at maximum extension (without locking out your joints) to get the most engagement with the muscle and then *slowly* lowering the weight back to its starting position.

You may also wish to alternate using weights with the latest trends in bodyweight exercises such as suspension training, animal movements and different crawling patterns to get the leanest, most athletic look possible while increasing your functional fitness.

As previously mentioned, mindful training, ie going slowly and using good form to connect the mind to the muscle, results in performance gains of an incredible 60% according to fitness trainer Steve Morgan, who gave me lots of great advice at my local gym. It's far more effective to drop the weight down but use great form while focusing on the specific muscle being worked than it is to use heavier weights but be sloppy about it.

Remember, the whole point of this Twelve-week Challenge is to continually find ways to train your mind–body connection so that when you're competing in a tournament, you can use this deep practice to bring your attention to your breathing, quieten your mind, reduce anxiety and allow your movement to flow.

Week Four

Congratulations, you are one-third of the way through your Twelve-week Challenge and it's time to look more closely at standing meditation, which was introduced in Part Two when, hopefully, you started your practice.

Of particular interest now is learning how we can use this advanced deep practice as a way to generate more power with less effort and to fully understand how all movement begins in the feet and therefore necessitates a strong and balanced lower body. This type of meditation is a prerequisite to many of the Kung Fu, Karate and other martial arts systems around the world and is considered basic training for beginner and advanced students alike.

As Mr Miyagi says in the *Karate Kid* movies, '*Balance is key. Balance good, karate good. Everything good. Balance bad, karate bad, better pack up, go home.*' We could apply this wisdom to many sports, and it often amazes me how little even professional or elite clients know about how to balance properly. Of course, few athletes spend time developing this as it's considered a given. In the martial arts, however, it's the be all and end all and is trained in isolation for many months and even years.

The famous Samurai swordsman Miyamoto Musashi, whom we met earlier, soundly beat each and every one of his opponents, not by practising sword forms and katas but by standing motionless for extended periods of time, training a state of relaxed readiness similar to that of a tiger poised to strike at its prey.

It might sound simple enough, but to stand motionless holding your body in a specific posture with your weight lowered into your legs and feet, your arms extended and your head held as if suspended from above requires enormous self-discipline and a certain type of resilience which goes beyond muscular endurance.

Standing practice will build a lot of strength in your legs, deep into the muscles and right through to your bone marrow, and it will develop your ability to balance like nothing else you've done. At the same time, however, it's important that you maintain a certain softness in the upper body so that your sporting movements can emerge naturally, from the ground upwards, even when you're under pressure.

To aid this, in Week Four you are going to begin working with the idea of stretching the fascia or connective tissue (see the action plan) to help keep your upper body loose, allowing it to follow the direction of the waist and impetus from the feet, thus developing greater connectivity and whole-body power. This will ensure you can move with greater ease while maintaining a stable base or foundation.

In addition to being the best form of balance training, standing practice is also a form of Chi Kung, as it has some incredible and well-documented health benefits. These include strengthening the bone marrow, which is where the body produces the red blood cells necessary to transport oxygen. It also decompresses the spinal column and enlivens the entire nervous system as well as helping to build reserves of Chi, or vital energy.

Before we go any further, here's a quick recap on what your weekly routine looks like now:

- You have your personal success soundtrack to listen to when you need a little encouragement or a reminder of the positive changes you have intended to make.

- If you have completed the action plan for Week Two, you will have made a vision board with powerful images that you've displayed somewhere you'll see them every day to help strengthen your resolve to stay strong and centred and to continue with your challenge.

- You will have adapted your daily routine to include meditation, the foundation of your Performance Practice, perhaps alternating the practice so you can now incorporate both seated and standing meditation.

- You will be maintaining a more mindful approach to eating, whether that's main meals, snacks or when mixing up a protein shake, and you'll be striving to maintain awareness of your breathing while enjoying your cardio workouts and keeping focused on the mind–muscle connection when training with weights.

Week Four action plan

Stretching the fascia

A fascia is a band or sheet of connective tissue, primarily collagen, beneath the skin that attaches, stabilises, encloses and separates muscles and other internal organs. It is classified by layer as superficial, deep, and visceral, or by its function and anatomical location.

Like ligaments and tendons, a fascia is made up of fibrous connective tissue containing closely packed bundles of collagen fibres oriented in a wavy pattern parallel to the direction of pull. Consequently, the fascia is flexible and able to resist enormous tension until such time as this potential force is released.

The increased power and explosiveness of using the fascia rather than sheer muscle power has long been known in Tai Chi, as this ancient quote attributed to the art's founder, Chang San-feng, and reproduced online by Michael P Garofalo, clearly shows:

> *'When you move upward, the mind must*
> *be aware of down;*
> *when moving forward, the mind also*
> *thinks of moving back;*
> *when shifting to the left side, the mind*
> *should simultaneously notice the right side,*
> *so that if the mind is going up,*
> *it is also going down.'*

Chi Performance works with the idea of opposing forces, which means stretching the fascia of the upper body away from the fascia of the lower body and stretching the fascia of the back while relaxing the front of the body. When standing, you are learning to create a conflict between the upper and lower body by emptying the chest to root into the legs while simultaneously raising the head and lengthening the spine, thus creating a structure that is strong yet pliable.

In Tai Chi terminology, your lower body is Yang (positive) and your upper body is Yin (negative), and these differing qualities are useful for helping athletes develop more potential energy without the need to use excessive force, thus reducing injuries. In your golf swing or tennis serve this will translate as a strong and grounded lower body combined with the spiral-like turning of a relaxed upper body through the centre of gravity, resulting in a feeling of greater connection and escalation (kinetic chain).

By stretching the fascia, you create an elastic potential which, when released, drives greater acceleration through the ball. Priming your body to wind up and emit centrifugal force by using the centre of gravity gives greater precision to your moves and ball striking.

To do

For the next week or so you might wish to experiment with how stretching the fascia can help you develop the condition of relaxed readiness when preparing for movement in your sport. For ideas to help you, please go back and review the slow-motion drills from Part Two.

In addition, you should be training your attention to reside in the t'an tien, thus enabling your breathing to deepen and slow down. This not only reduces anxiety and mental interference, as we've seen, but also opens the communication channels between your mind and body, helping your movement to flow more freely.

Some advanced work being done in the field of physio-therapy even suggests that the fascia is the transmitter of light and consciousness through the physical body, which would go some way to explaining the explosive nature of a Kung Fu punch that responds instanta-neously to intention, which operates at a far greater speed than the thinking mind with its checklists and menus of movement positions.

Weeks Five To Eight

Over the next four weeks you're going to start deeper work on Key Six – activation of the t'an tien. As we've noted, this area is also known as the hara centre in Yoga and Zazen, and I've heard swimmers refer to it as 'the zero point'. You will also go deeper into your standing practice with some advanced guidelines (see the action plan).

As we've seen, the t'an tien is your body's natural centre of gravity, and many athletes feel this centre working when they are relaxed and in the zone; for instance, on a smooth drive off the first tee or during an effortless strike of the baseball. As biomechanics includes little or no instruction about this, it can be difficult, if not impossible, to understand what's taking place and how to replicate it, so let's look at this more closely from our Eastern perspective.

Imagine this area as a small ball, perhaps the size of a golf or tennis ball, around which the upper body or torso can turn quite freely *without* disturbing the structure and balance of the lower body. This means that by using the centre of gravity, we can understand human motion in three dimensions, and athletes can employ it to get more torque and acceleration when using a bat, club or racket and to initiate spin in more expressive sports like snowboarding, gymnastics or ice skating.

Strictly speaking, the upper body should never initiate movement but should simply respond to signals or instructions given by the pressure of the feet in contact with the ground and by the centre of gravity, which in turn guides the waist and propels the arms.

During weeks Five, Six, Seven and Eight of your Twelve-week Challenge, you can continue to practise any of your sporting moves in slow motion, making sure to stay rooted in your feet and keep your upper body relaxed while freely rotating around this imaginary ball. You will then feel how the t'an tien resolves the polarity between being grounded and stable while remaining loose and relaxed, as your body can express the kinetic chain in a way that is perfectly connected and unimpeded by the thinking mind, which only serves to segment movement.

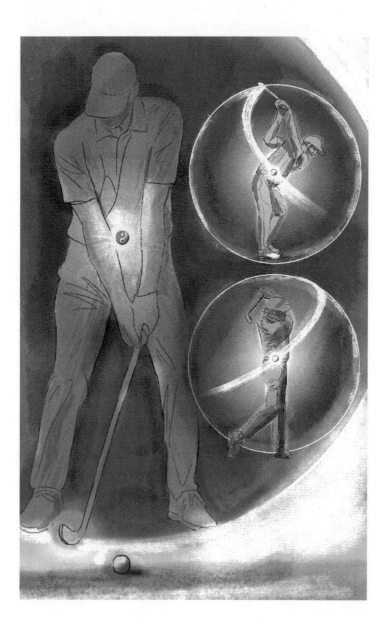

The Tai Chi concept of movement being rooted in the feet, springing from the legs, guided by the waist and expressed in the hands is the most biomechanically efficient way to move the body for effortless power and precision and helps train your sporting movements in a way that encourages the activation of TMB.

Now that your Twelve-week Challenge has been fully outlined and you've made a great start on bringing positive changes into your daily routine and your preparations for elevating your performance under pressure, you will simply continue to work the plan day by day until the end of the challenge.

You may find that you have less mental interference now than when you started, as you continually make the effort to connect in the most fundamental way to your body and breathing.

When you're next in contention, having honed and practised what's necessary to stay quiet inside, free of negative thoughts and anxiety, your body will naturally release your movement skills in a way that surpasses your current level of performance and brings increased enjoyment to your sport.

Weeks Five to Eight action plan

Review and continue

Please continue to work the plan over the next four weeks; this is when most people will tail off, as the default human tendency is to make less and less effort over time.

If necessary, review the notes in your journal and remind yourself of all the reasons why you embarked on this Twelve-week Challenge. Was it to get better at your sport? How specifically? Was it to be able to perform under pressure instead of letting anxiety ruin your chance of winning? Was it to change your dietary habits, lose weight or overcome an injury? What are the changes you want to see? Was it to develop a more athletic physique? How is that showing up for you?

It's worthwhile spending some time going over your initial plan, which will include your personal goals in each of the Eight Keys to Mind–Body Training.

Feel free to adapt, change and alter your original goals as you approach the next four weeks. With your newly found inner quietude and a sense of being more relaxed in life and sport, you may find that things you once held as important are no longer so pressing, while goals you thought you might never reach seem closer than ever.

In his book *The Art of Expressing the Human Body*, the legendary Kung Fu fighter and movie star, Bruce Lee, wrote about the importance of regularly reviewing one's training regime to 'sharpen and dissolve' – that is, tighten up what's most in keeping with your developing potential while allowing everything else to fall away.

Advanced standing practice

When standing in meditation, use the guidelines in Principle Four: Relaxed Readiness, with the following additions to deepen your practice:

1. When you begin, you need to place your body in the correct position, with the proper skeletal alignments (or as close as you can manage).

2. Throughout the practice session, old postural habits will come back into play, but through awareness and conscious effort you can retrain these habits and improve them over time.

3. As your posture gets closer to ideal (one that can let the force of gravity sink down through the legs and into the feet), less stress is placed on the musculature, and the body and mind can both relax. The musculature of our bodies can, broadly speaking, be divided into two categories: postural and phasic. The postural muscles, as the name implies, deal with holding the skeleton in

position, and they naturally have more strength and endurance than the phasic muscles.

4. Standing exercises help us to relax the musculature while still maintaining a strong frame, aiming to minimise the use of the phasic muscles and maximise the use of the postural muscles. The better we can become at doing this, the more we can maintain a strong structure and remain reasonably relaxed. A strong structure is one that can receive and/or emit force and still maintain its shape.

Weeks Nine,
Ten And Eleven

For the next three weeks you're going to continue to work the plan, tightening up your focus to bring the mind and body together in all your activities, from your meditation to how you eat and exercise and during your sports training sessions.

It is *always* possible to go deeper into the relationship between stillness and motion, from where we can potentially access the zone, or flow state, which renders complex movement effortless, so please keep on keeping on.

You might also like to review and update your success soundtrack, your vision board and your affirmations to acknowledge the positive changes you've made so far. Keep writing up your triumphs, observations and weekly plan every Sunday in your journal and continue planning for the week ahead.

Keep going – you're nearly there!

You're almost at the finish of your Twelve-week Challenge. As many others who've already been through this process have realised, this new way of living and training for fitness, physique development and sports performance, which is based entirely around the all-important mind–body connection, is something you'll want to keep in place long after the challenge has ended.

Together we've looked at the Eight Keys to Mind–Body Training, which I've identified over three decades of using Eastern principles and practices to help those who love sport understand and train what's necessary to deliver fluid, powerful, effortless and precise motion when they are under pressure.

We've examined the role these eight keys play in bringing mind and body together so you can become the best athletic version of yourself to date and be prepared to play your sport in a way that enhances both your enjoyment and performance levels.

You now have a better plan for your diet, nutrition, hydration and supplementation, and doubtless you are leaner and fitter than you were twelve weeks ago.

If you continue with this work, your physique will only get better.

You have ramped up your cardiovascular and conditioning workouts, not only varying between tempo, slow burn and high-intensity interval training for a healthier heart and maximum fat loss, but you're also learning how to focus your attention on your breathing so that you can increase your oxygen uptake, train for longer and recover more quickly.

You have been incorporating fascia stretching based on Tai Chi philosophy, developing upper-body softness that encourages the torso to follow the movement of your waist without disturbing your balance. This training will help you release natural movement when you're under pressure, as it adheres to the fundamental laws of human motion, which predate sports science and biomechanics by many hundreds of years.

You have also learned how to develop lower-body strength and stability, which modern sports science calls 'ground force energy' or 'vertical force'. It is a way to generate power from the ground rather than using brute muscular force, thus requiring less effort and keeping you safe from avoidable injuries.

Over these past weeks, I've sought to bring you a fail-safe approach to staying strong and centred and doing all the necessary practice and preparation for being in the now when you're next under pressure. This training has been necessary to help you overcome the biochemical reactions to stress, which include rushing, overthinking and trying too hard.

Having practised seated and standing meditation for almost three months, you are now able to bring a quiet inner focus to your pre-shot, pre-routine or dismount preparations without letting nerves, anxiety or mental interference disrupt your focus.

This Twelve-week Mind–Body Performance Challenge is unlike anything else currently available in the health and fitness or sports performance markets. We have looked at how to activate your body's centre of gravity to generate spin, torque, increased rotation and acceleration, enabling the most complex of sporting movements to be performed in a way that is fluid and yet still precise.

Perhaps most importantly of all, you have built a routine where you've incorporated traditional, formal seated and standing meditation to help quieten the mind, develop relaxed power and allow access to the present moment.

Finally, let's look at raising your Chi, which is a concept thousands of years old and based on various methods of the Eastern world, known collectively as Chi Kung.

Weeks Nine, Ten and Eleven action plan

Energy gains

To build energy reserves, most athletes have to be content with getting the right food and supplements and enough rest, but you now have a process to cultivate your internal energy (Chi) with attention control, abdominal (navel) breathing and standing meditation, which all provide additional performance gains to give you the edge over your competitors. You are learning that:

- Eating more slowly and consciously helps you extract the maximum amount of energy from your meals and snacks

- Lower abdominal breathing increases your oxygen uptake and aids relaxation, thus saving valuable energy which would otherwise be wasted through anxiety and mental interference

- Letting your mind rest at the t'an tien helps set the shoulders down, empty your chest and relax your waist to encourage the energy to settle at your body's physical centre of gravity

- Chi can be stored in the lower t'an tien and thus be employed to give greater force to your kicks, jumps and ball striking and also to prevent illness by developing internal strength and resilience

T'an tien breathing

To help store the Chi in your lower t'an tien, you might like to try t'an tien breathing. After sitting quietly for a short while, breathe in and out through the nose and when you exhale concentrate on pushing some of the breath down into the t'an tien. Of course, the breath does not actually move to the lower abdomen, but concentration on the t'an tien will help you to produce a composed and concentrated state of mind and feel stronger physically. Go easy with this exercise – it's powerful, so you only need to practise for a few minutes each time you're sitting in meditation.

Many clients have reported that adopting this practice when playing sport helps them to produce more power in their golf swing, tennis serves etc.

Week Twelve

Congratulations! You have now joined an elite category of those who have stayed the course over twelve long weeks. You have been consistent with your focus on staying strong and centred and remembering to come back to the present moment, thus preparing for a marked ascent in your athletic performance and enjoyment. That puts you in the top 10% of all those who lead an active lifestyle.

It's time to write up your achievements, perhaps take a full-length photo of yourself to add to your vision board and make time to celebrate the completion of your Twelve-week Mind–Body Performance Challenge in whatever way you feel is appropriate.

Don't forget to share the news and relay a big thank you to all those who have helped, supported and encouraged you since you first shared your goals and aspirations with them in Week One.

You might also like to make a detailed plan of how you can take this new approach to mind–body fitness and performance into the remainder of the year or in preparation for an upcoming season.

Well done!

Please get in touch through the website if you would like to share your triumph with me and my team and receive your Twelve-week Mind–Body Performance Challenge certificate of completion.

Conclusion

The mind–body connection is the new frontier in sports performance. However, I am not of the belief that this approach will ever entirely replace technical and mental game coaching, as these have their role and designated place in your development as an athlete. I do believe, though, that the time has come to make a distinction between what's needed in terms of the training required to learn and hone complex movement, and what's necessary during high-pressure situations like tournaments and other competitive events – indeed, in the moments before you begin your routine or strike the ball – in order to freely express and release this movement in a way that is natural and spontaneous.

The overarching message of this book is that the athlete's preparedness to enter the zone or flow state can be trained alongside fitness and athletic prowess, but the caveat is that it can only be trained using principles and practices that go beyond the physical, mechanical and even the psychological. These principles and practices have long been known in the Eastern world of the martial and meditative arts, and many of them have been set out for you in this book. They are as simple and yet as challenging as they were for the devotees, spiritual seekers and warriors of the ancient past.

Your ascent as an athlete, and with it your enjoyment of the sport you love, can only occur when you incorporate this centuries-old approach alongside the mental and technical components of modern-day sports performance – when you develop the twin states of inner quietude and relaxed readiness alongside confidence in your abilities and a keen understanding of your craft. If you think, as many coaches and players still tend to do, that the mind–body connection is a given, and that we can apply the same approach as we do to 'thinking about thinking' and 'thinking about movement', then this path is not for you, even if you have enjoyed the book and concur with much of what's been said. The inherent danger, given the world in which we live and the level of awareness with which most people operate, is to believe that you can somehow attain the mind–body connection through a concentrated effort of thinking, a two-minute meditation practice or the use of an app.

This is a road that cannot lead far. It certainly isn't a path you can journey along for a lifetime, forever uncovering more layers of the extraordinary presence that exists within and above each one of us, and which is responsible for the breath, life and movement in our bodies.

It's true that after many long years I may be further along this path, but I am still on the way, as are my team of coaches. Each of us strives to practise, day after day, the techniques that have been shown in this book. We're ready to help you, guide you and teach you what we know, but you must be ready to embrace real quietude without distractions or excuses, without grasping or forcing. Thus, you will develop a relaxed self-awareness, which, when it manifests on the tennis or basketball court, at the top of the ski run, on the first tee, by the poolside or as you start your routine on the floor mat or ice rink, will render your experience of sport and the creative self-expression of the body truly sublime.

Next steps

I offer bespoke one-to-one coaching programmes for competitive amateur athletes wishing to break through performance barriers and for elite athletes and professionals to help them master high-pressure situations and enjoy more wins. My team of accredited coaches offer introductory coaching programmes.

Training is currently available online and in person in the UK, France and Sweden. To find out more about our programmes or express an interest in joining our European coaching team, get in touch via the website at www.chi-performance.com.

Bibliography

Ancona, D and Chon CL, 'Entrainment: Cycles and synergy in organizational behavior', working paper (July 1992), https://dspace.mit.edu/bitstream/handle/1721.1/2421/swp-3443-26943587.pdf?sequence=1, accessed 26 January 2024

Ashe, A and Deford, F, *Arthur Ashe: Potrait in motion* (Houghton Mifflin, 1975)

Aurobindo, S, *The Integral Yoga: Sri Aurobindo's teaching and method of practice* (Lotus Press, 1993)

Aurobindo, S, *The Synthesis of Yoga* (Lotus Press, 1992)

Canfield, J, *Success Principles* (HarperCollins, 2005)

Chuen, L, *The Way of Power* (Gaia, 2005)

Clark, N, *Sports Nutrition Guidebook* (Human Kinetics, 2019)

Csikszentmihalyi, M, *Flow: The psychology of optimal experience* (Rider, 2002)

Diepersloot, J, *Warriors of Stillness* (Diepersloot, 1995)

DonsHooplifesports, 'Kobe Bryant thoughts on Steph Curry', YouTube Shorts (13 April 2021), www.youtube.com/shorts/r-06h4mSRc0, accessed 26 January 2024

Gallop, R, *The G.I. (Glycaemic Index) Diet* (Workman Publishing, 2010)

Garofalo, MP, 'Chang San-Feng: Taoist grand master, circa 1200 CE' (Green Way Research, 2020), www.egreenway.com/taichichuan/chang1.htm, accessed 26 January 2024

Garfield, O, *The Original Mediterranean Diet Cookbook* (Independently published, 2019)

Gurdjieff, GI, *Views from the Real World: Early talks of Gurdjieff as recollected by his pupils* (Paul H Crompton, 2012)

Harung, H and Travis, F, *World-Class Brain: The edge that helps peak performers succeed and how you can develop it* (Harvest AS, 2020)

Hilton, C, *Inside the Mind of the Grand Prix Driver* (J H Haynes & Co Ltd, 2001)

Heathcote, F, *Peak Performance: Zen and the sporting zone* (Merlin Publishing, 1996)

Iyengar, BKS, *Light on the Yoga Sutras of Patanjali* (Thorsons 1996)

Kammer, R, *Zen and Confucius in the Art of Swordsmanship: The 'Tengu-geijutsu-ron' of Chozan Shissai* (Routledge, 1978, ebook published 2016)

Lee, B, *The Art of Expressing the Human Body* (Tuttle Publishing, 1998)

Mahoney, JF, *Tao of the Jump Shot* (Ulysses Press, 2000)

Musashi, M, *A Book of Five Rings* (CreateSpace Independent Publishing Platform, 2012)

Phillips, B, *Body for Life* (William Morrow, 2003)

Stein, H, *Kyudo: The art of zen archery* (Element Books, 1998)

Suzuki, S, *Zen Mind, Beginner's Mind* (Shambhala Publications Inc, 2020)

Wayne, PM and Fuerst, ML, *The Harvard Medical School Guide to Tai Chi: 12 weeks to a healthy body, strong heart, and sharp mind* (Shambhala Publications, 2013)

Yellin, S and Biancalana, B, *The 7 Secrets of World Class Athletes* (CreateSpace Independent Publishing Platform, 2010)

Acknowledgements

With grateful thanks to Tess Jolly for her sensitive and thoughtful editing. To Ryan, Mike and Stirling for their generous help with funding, and to Tom Harding for creating beautiful illustrations that really capture the message of the book.

The Author

Jayne Storey is the founder and head coach of Chi Performance and the author of several books, including *Breathe Golf: The missing link to a winning performance* (Panoma Press, 2019). Her background includes thirty-seven years' training in formal Buddhist meditation and various martial arts styles, including Tai Chi.

Jayne's unique approach to sports performance uses simple principles of centuries-old mind–body disciplines to help athletes develop a Performance Practice to overcome anxiety, nerves and mental interference. Her approach has formed part of the PGA's Member Education Programme, and her accreditation syllabus is endorsed by WellBeing Insurance.

Jayne has written instructional articles for a number of sporting publications, including *Golf International*, *Atlantic Golf & Lifestyle*, *Kingdom*, *Women's Golf Journal* and *Sports Coach*, and she has been featured on BBC television and radio as well as numerous podcasts.

Jayne is a member of the Tai Chi Union for Great Britain and also trains with the Kalarippayat Academy UK. In her leisure time, she enjoys visiting the ancient temples in Malta and playing Latin guitar.

⊕ www.chi-performance.com

Also by Jayne Storey

Breathe Golf: The missing link to a winning performance
(Panoma Press, 2019)

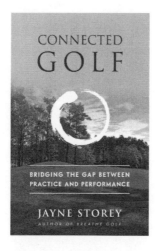

Connected Golf: Bridging the gap between practice and performance (Panoma Press, 2022)